An Interview With So...
Joy Hendry

JH: Sorley, you are now established as probably the foremost poet writing in any language in Scotland today. What started you writing poetry?

SM: I'm not sure what really started me. I was fond of poetry of all kinds from the age of 14 onwards, but I think I was even fonder of old Gaelic song, and I consider the fusion of poetry and music in those Gaelic songs as it were the very last word in what the Gaels have done. And there was a kind of impotence about me in the sense that I couldn't sing. I was one of the few of our family who couldn't sing or play the pipes or something like that, but I was passionately fond of it.

I read all kinds of poetry from a fairly early age. A lot of bad stuff to begin with - Scott's metrical romances and William Edmonstoune Aytoun, but I graduated to better things. I had a passion for Shelley for a while, but I don't think my verse was ever influenced by Shelley in form. It was, I think, (influenced) by Blake and Wordsworth. I have great admiration for Wordsworth. Of the Gaelic poets, I think William Ross, but for a while MacDonald and MacIntyre, who are so different from Ross and from each other.

JH: When you started writing as a teenager and as an undergraduate, it was English you were writing in, wasn't it?

SM: No, I was writing Gaelic as well as English, but at about the age of 20 I destroyed all I could lay hands on of my English poetry. You see I had written a poem called 'The Heron' when I was comparatively young - 20, or perhaps only 19 - and I realised it was better than anything I had done in English. And there were what you might call patriotic reasons: I was obsessed with the probable demise of Gaelic, and I shuddered to think of a day when the great Gaelic songs could not be heard properly because there wouldn't be people to speak the language. Economic reasons made me take a degree in English rather than in Celtic, but I don't think that was a bad thing at all, fundamentally.

JH: It gave you breadth?

SM: It gave me a breadth; and I doubt whether, if one is to be a poet writing in English, one should take a degree in English. Norman MacCaig is very strong on that, and I'm inclined to agree with him.

JH: Several famous Scottish poets haven't gone to university at all.

SM: Of course, of course.

JH: To come back to the old songs, why are they so superlative?

SM: Because they are a fusion of music with poetry. They have great passion and brevity, but they have also evocations of things like landscape and so on which make them different from the old Scottish ballads which I admire greatly. They are rarely stark, but they are sometimes; and they have a great authority. There are so many of them.

JH: I think you said somewhere that your ambition was to equal their achievement in verse. Do you think you've done that?

SM: Oh God, no! I don't think I had great ambitions about verse at all. In many ways I consider in my verse that I was a kind of musician *manqué*.
JH: So it was your inability to sing that spurred you into poetry?
SM: Well, I'm not sure - it's awfully difficult - it was something to do with that. You see, I have a great liking for Virgil, for instance. We were taught Latin superbly. I hadn't read Catullus when I young, but had a great liking for Virgil and some of the 19th century French poets, like Baudelaire and Verlaine.
JH: Really, your Gaelic poetry is drawing on a wide European basis?
SM: I suppose in a way it is, but I would say that fundamentally my roots are more Gaelic than anything else.
JH: Do you see yourself as part of the Bardic tradition, rather than a poet as an individual? I think English poets and probably Lowland Scottish poets see themselves very much as individuals. But do you see yourself as less of an individual and more part of a continuing tradition?
SM: No I wouldn't say that. I am, in a way, in a continuing tradition, but I wouldn't say that lessens my individuality. I hope it doesn't.
JH: Do you see yourself as a Bard, in that community sense?
SM: In certain of my poems I do; in many others I do not.
JH: Can you name a poem in which you do see yourself working as a bard?
SM: Well actually, that early one, 'The Ship'. It's ... one of the few poems I've ever 'sat down' to write, and there was a kind of deliberation in the symbols of that poem. And it referred to things in the Gaelic tradition - the verse of the great 18th century poets like MacDonald and MacIntyre and others; and the old songs, where the black ship is fundamentally a reference to the black ships of Clan Ronald in Alexander MacDonald, and the white one (referring to) the old songs. I had a kind of impotent rage about the improvement of the old songs, because very often I couldn't properly do anything about it myself because I couldn't sing. My sisters could, and my brothers ...
JH: ... and your Auntie Peggy ...
SM: My Auntie Peggy was wonderful, and I remember my own paternal grandmother before that, and certain of my Nicolson relations. Though I didn't hear them often, my uncle Angus Nicolson was a wonderfully good singer, but I didn't get a chance of hearing him often then.
JH: So your poetry is very much informed by this rich tradition of poetry and music seen as more or less a seamless garment.
SM: Yes, I would say so. Of course you must remember that up to this century, practically all Gaelic poetry was for singing, or chanting in the case of the old Ossianic and Fingalian and Red Branch Lays.
JH: So this qualitative distinction between poetry and song is rather a bourgeois 19th century phenomenon?
SM: Well, I wouldn't go to the length of saying that. I was impressed by the common thesis of Professor Herbert Grierson that the lyric, the real lyric in a way suggested song even if it weren't set to music at all. And that was reinforced by a reading of (Benedetto) Croce.
JH: To shift territory slightly, one of the remarkable things about your poetry that appeals to many people, is that you take what is really

intense private experience and transmute it into poetry, which is a public statement. For instance, family circumstances prevented you from fighting in the Spanish Civil War, and you have chosen to write about that intimately in your poetry. Why? It seems to me a brave thing to do in a way, to expose your innermost thoughts to such public scrutiny.

SM: Well, yes, I would say that my poetry is not propagandist so much as confessional. My quarrel is fundamentally with myself, not with the outside world. A lot of things were intensified and accelerated by the likelihood of war in the thirties. It wasn't so much the war I was afraid of, but of Europe being taken over by German fascism, German Nazism, and being a kind of pessimist, I fully expected that as things were going it was likely that there would be a thousand years of Nazi domination, which was racist too, you know. And that worked in with my Scottish nationalism because the Nazis regarded the English as more Teutonic than the Scots. And that affected me very much. And, as you know - or perhaps you don't know - I asked Edinburgh Corporation to release me for the army on the second day of the war.

JH: So in poems like 'The Cry of Europe' and 'The Choice' it is really yourself you are taking to task?

SM: Well, in a way, I am taking myself to task. In 1936-7 a woman did not keep me from Spain, but I realised that if it were a pure choice between the woman and Spain, I would choose the woman.

JH: Yes, that brings us on quite naturally to your love poetry. You have known several women who feature strongly in that poetry. Are there not problems about that, in that people take the sequence as being too much biographical in nature?

SM: Well, it's not really a sequence. The only part that could be called a sequence at all is that part called *The Haunted Ebb*. And there is practically no confict there. It doesn't have a conflict in my opinion, very little conflict, but it is actually a tragic situation which lasted from December '39 until about August '41, and was followed by a period of grave perplexity. And all this was accentuated by the fact that for a lot of that period I was in the army . . .

JH: . . . that's right, in the North African Desert . . .

SM: And, I suppose, in many ways I regarded myself as a failed man of action. And in the army I actually volunteered in 1941 for a parachutist's job, and then for a direct transfer to the Camerons, which I thought would be more dangerous than the Signals. I missed that by a day, I found out recently.

JH: So you wanted to be in the front line?

SM: Yes, but I found out that the Signals could be in the front line too. I was hit thrice, actually. But you see, after August 1941, it wasn't a kind of suicidal business that drove me. I continued after that to want to be in a dangerous job. Of course, my experience of the British army is that if ever there was a call for volunteers there would be twenty times more volunteers than could be taken. I must say that, for the kind of men who were with me in the Signals.

JH: So there was a suicidal element to your wanting to be in the front line as

well as your desire to be a man of action.
SM: Well there was, before August '41.
JH: So how did it change then?
SM: It changed because the personal tragedy turned out not to be a tragedy.
JH: But you have always used the impetus which comes from emotional crisis to write. You are not someone who writes habitually. You don't sit down at your desk every morning and do a couple of hours.
SM: Oh no. No.
JH: You write very much out of emotional crises.
SM: I have ... I have very often, but I think there is a considerable variety in my verse, just as there is a very big variety in form.
JH: You mentioned form. You have to an extent revolutionised Gaelic poetry in the 20th century. People see you as having introduced elements like surrealism and all kinds of stylistic influences from outside the Gaelic world.
SM: Yes, and also, you see, the fact that Gaelic assonances come into my verse doesn't mean that it is a kind of following of tradition, because nobody has ever been able to tell me where the rhythm of, for instance, a thing like 'Kinloch Ainort' has come from. And, of course, even those of the war poems like 'An Autumn Day' and 'Death Valley', and there are quite a few more, and one of the parts of 'The Woods of Raasay'. Nobody has ever been able to tell me - at least nobody whose opinion I would consider of any importance.
JH: Do you know where the rhythm comes from yourself?
SM: No. I don't know, and I have often been asked, specially with regard to 'The Cry of Europe'. It may have a lot of assonances, and things like that; and 'Kinloch Ainort'. I just don't know, and I don't know where at all ... at all where it comes from. There is nothing that I know of in Gaelic - and I know Gaelic verse pretty well, you see: I used to have a very retentive memory.
JH: If MacDiarmid dragged Scottish poetry - certainly poetry in Scots - into the 20th century, do you think you did that for Gaelic poetry?
SM: That is really a big question to ask me, and I think that you should ask other people, I mean not everybody, but other people.
JH: You mentioned earlier Shelley, and you've also the fate of Gaeldom as being for you almost a political spur. What else was it that shaped your political ideals? On the one hand you are a firmly committed socialist, as you have been all your life; and you are also a very strong nationalist. Who were the main political influences? John MacLean, perhaps?
SM: Well, you see, I think in the influence of John MacLean was perhaps a bit of ignorance in the romantic attitude some held of him, because I met quite a few people who either knew him or were followers of him. Of course I was influenced by MacDiarmid himself in that way. He was, to me, such a self-sacrificing person, politically. But, I don't think he had much influence on me politically.
JH: History did, though. I mean the fate of Gaeldom, the Clearances ...
SM: Yes, yes. Not only the fate of history, but the fate of so much that had happened in the world. You see I don't think I was ever a full-blown

Sorley MacLean as student, Edinburgh, early 1930s

Marxist, in the sense that I accepted completely a materialist or, even to a great extent, a materialist philosophy. But history made me realise that Marx had made some valid generalisations about the fate of the great bulk of humanity, and I still believe that to this day.

JH: One of the stones against which you have honed your Socialist axe, if you like, has been the Clearances. Am I right in thinking that you have seen that as very much perpetrated by right-wing philosophies?

SM: Yes, I have, in a way, but you see perhaps I was too much inclined to consider those right-wing philosophies too much as a product of economic circumstances . . . and on the other hand, I always much affected, even at a very early age, by what was happening in lowland Scotland, and even in England you know. I was very passionate - I was only 14 - about the General Strike of 1926, the long strike of the miners, because, apart from the Clearances, there were so many people that we could come into touch with, that came home at the Glasgow Fair and all that. There was a man quite unconnected with me who had some poor job on the Clyde, and he used to perhaps come to Raasay for a week in the year and stay with relatives. The attitude of people like him to John MacLean was that he was a great god to them. Now he was not a colleague or a relative of mine in the least . . .

And of course, although Edinburgh hadn't the slums that Glasgow had - not so many - it had some very, very bad ones. Remember, that was 1929, and I was in Edinburgh during the great slump, which was at its height in 1931 and 1932. I was very much affected by the success of the so-called 'National Government' of 1931. I considered that a dreadful business. Perhaps I was wrong in thinking that Nazism was purely a thing that came from the landlord/capitalist class. I may have - I probably did - minimise the purely nationalist, racialist, populist quality in it.

JH: Some critics - I think particularly English critics - tend to regard it as bad manners to mix poetry and politics. Obviously you've had no problem with that because your poetry is full of politics.

SM: Yes, but I don't think I'm a propagandist. I think my quarrel is mainly . . . I think on the whole, the quarrel is mainly myself.

JH: How do you get above that level of propaganda, into what is genuinely political poetry? What is the difference between these two things?

SM: . . . Well, you see, my poetry is fundamentally a criticism of myself, and given situations, rather than an exaltation of any particular cause - well, that's how I find it at any rate.

JH: And so the politics emerges almost in a dramatic way out of the poetry.

SM: I think so. And at any rate, an awful lot of poetry is bad manners in one way - in fact it has almost got to be bad manners I would say.

JH: In what way?

SM: If it is honest, it has to be frank. And very often frankness is bad manners. Very often I regret the taking of certain people as examples, I'm afraid I was influenced in that by the practice of Hugh MacDiarmid, who scarified people in public about whom he was quite kind in private - well I don't think I did that, but I think . . . Sydney Smith used to say, "No stiff upper lip for Smith!" I howled like a wolf.

JH: Can we switch again now to poetry readings. A lot of people have said to me that there's something ironic about the fact that people do flock in the lowlands to hear you reading - people who have no understanding of Gaelic whatsoever. Does this bother you in any way?

SM: No. It fundamentally doesn't bother me at all.

JH: I mean to what extent can these people appreciate your poetry, given that they are hearing only the English translation?

SM: Ah, but they are actually hearing the sound of the Gaelic as well. And I don't know, you see, but my reading is rather . . . what is the word I want? It's not 'deliberate' . . .

JH: You're thinking about the way in which you intone your verse?

SM: Well, the point is, fundamentally, I do not believe that poetry is a purely naturalistic art. I don't believe in what you might call a naturalistic reading. There must be a kind of compromise, I think, between the speech - the normal sounds of the speech - and metrical forms.

JH: So you're quite sanguine, really, about the ablity of somebody who knows only the English to get at least a good grip of what you are saying through the English translation?

SM: Well, I read the English translation first, usually, to give people an idea of what I am talking about. I think fundamentally, to me at any rate, and to all Gaels, the sensuousness of Gaelic poetry - the primary one, I should say - is to the ear.

JH: Arising out of that question, Sorley, is there a critical problem with regard to your work, and indeed the work of any Gaelic poet? Many people have made great claims for your work, have said that you are a great poet in the European tradition, and so on. But actually there are very few people who know Gaelic at all, or well enough to make a proper critical judgment on that?

SM: Well, I'd say this: the greatest claims, the most extravagant claims that have been made for my stuff is by native Gaelic-speaking Gaels. And of course, you must remember there are quite a lot of people now in Scotland, who have quite a lot of Gaelic without being native speakers.

JH: Yes, I know several people who have actually learnt Gaelic in order to be able to read your poetry in the original.

SM: Yes, well I've heard that said . . .

JH: So, are you therefore quite sanguine about the future of Gaelic?

SM: Well, nowadays I am more sanguine than I was. I think Gaelic will survive, if it is only after a fashion that it will survive. But there is happening, at present, the wonderful success of Gaelic medium primary teaching, which I am acquainted with in places like Portree School. Of course, at present there are so few taking advantage of that. But when you hear people, neither of whose parents are Gaelic, speaking Gaelic quite naturally . . . but there are comparatively few such Gaelic-medium classes although they are increasing. There is also bi-lingual teaching, which gets in more, but is not so successful as the Gaelic-medium teaching is with a few . . . a comparative few.

JH: You yourself have fought in the realm of education for certain reforms, like the introduction of a Gaelic learners' paper.

SM: Yes. I think I did more for that than anybody except Donald Thomson, Donald Morrison, and my brother John. We were the vocal people for it. And I probably brought the thing out into the open in the early 60s.

JH: You regard that as a great personal achievement, don't you.

SM: Well, in a way, not really. I am glad that I did a lot to reinforce what people like Donald Thomson, Donald Morrison in Oban, and my brother John, were doing - there were others too, particularly, I would say, teachers of three-year schools in Argyllshire. And what the Glasgow Labour Corporation did in what was originally two secondary schools. Perhaps I was rather rough in my methods in that . . .

JH: But you got the results.

SM: . . . and offended what I would call the 'some-place Gaels' or 'platform Gaels'.

JH: So, a last question, then, Sorley, about teaching. For years you taught as a teacher of English, then as a principal teacher of English, and then as a headmaster. How did you manage to reconcile that with your poetry?

SM: Well, economic necessity. But also, I taught Gaelic after 4.00pm, and even at Boroughmuir School for years. And for sixteen years, I was not only head teacher of Plockton School, but I was assistant teacher of Gaelic, and for some years I taught practically all the Gaelic including . . . and that was at a time when, in Plockton School, there was only one out of ten who I would call a native speaker, and that was before the Learners' Paper came in in 1968.

JH: But it did certainly draw on a lot of energy that could otherwise have been going into your writing, didn't it?

SM: Actually, I have seen myself in Plockton School teaching forty periods out of forty-five in the week, and being dead tired. You see, if I had been a better teacher, I wouldn't have taken so much out of myself as I did, but that of course is a matter . . . well, difficult to assess. And a lot of nervous energy went into propaganda, because I was saying in public what people like Donald Thomson, Donald Morrison, and my brother John would say in private. There are difficulties about that.

JH: But you have been retired now for some years, and able to take your place as a Scottish Man of Letters, as it were. Are you still writing now, and if so, what are you writing about?

SM: For the last year I haven't been doing very much actual writing. I've been taken up with a lot of other things. This business of having to translate is a very difficult thing too, because, whereas I don't consider those translations as it were final, because if I think of a better phrase or word in a given instance, then I will use it.

JH: But it is very much an ongoing work, even, like producing final versions of the Cuillin, which you wrote many years ago, for publication in *Chapman*. Anyway, Sorley, can I just say thank you for speaking to us today. It's been a marvellous hour. (SM goes on to read 'The Cry of Europe' and 'Kinloch Ainort')

The complete text of an interview broadcast on Radio Scotland, 25 July, 1989, producer Bruce Young.

John Welch

OVERLOOKING THE LOCH (OBAN, SCOTLAND)

This is the kind of mist
that drives people indoors to their Scotch.
Stinging and swarming,
it blinds the sheep and
butts heads with the stones.
Even the gulls protest,
beating home through air
like uncarded wool,
snarled with smoke
from peat and hearth and tea.
The winds have taken cover
like everything else; they
go burrowing down the grasses
like mice beneath a rug.
One breaks for the loch
and the mist pounces.
The little wind dies
with its back to the water,
squealing and clawing
with desperate feet.

ON A JETTY JUTTING INTO THE ATLANTIC

Deep in the nap of your jacket
my fingers are roots
clawing away from the wind

a moderate gale
that cuts at the waves
like a plane blading wood.

Shavings of sand and spray
curl up together
blond and raw in the sun

only to falter and fall
spent, as you said,
like us

glory bent slowly
drift and dust.

THREE FACES AND SKY

1.

I am a boy named Matthew
smeared with the smell
of my mother's mint
that grew, until now,
beside the back door.
They have already called
me for supper twice, but
I stand on the stoop
where the wind chime bangs
and bend over backwards
until all I see is sky
suddenly close
stupendously blue
barren of all but the
muscae volitantes in my eyes
drifting across it like indolent eels.
My name, as big for me as
my father's hat, slides
deliberately
off.

2.

I am a woman, parting
the curtain at dusk
for someone who hasn't come.
Halfway down the sky
the new moon hangs as it does
when it's cold and very clear
hanging and waiting
stoking itself against cannibal night.
Smudged and unignited world!
Things writhe and die
until the earth spurts grief
like a ruptured orange.
Turn, then. I need to turn
on these ghouls of mine.
I will harry them with
raving teeth, my eyes
like owls' on rodent fear,
my hair a torch to beat back
the night, the match
that sets the moon aflame.

3.

I am old and have rocked
on the porch since noon.
I never wasted time
until it wasted me.
But now I just watch as pigeons
malcontent with their favourite eaves
wheel in the sunset, trailing light.
And I remember - late May,
shadows of the bare young grass
dally across her ankles,
almost as young and just as bare.
And always, it seems, I wait
an elderly bubble that leans and yearns,
poised on the plastic wand of a child.
The wind trembles, and I want to go.
I want to cruise the last light
darting it back in reds and blues
to be above it all
lucid
and free.

MT PHILO

Four days now
the wind ringing
the boughs of these pines
raking the stones
of silence.

Four days and
still it goes on
the piling up, the crumbling away
almost an architecture aimed at the ear
almost inaudible, the way
time passes.

Surely something like this
was the tiny whispering sound
that soothed the face of the mountain
when the windstorm, the earthquake,
the fireburst had passed
when Elijah hid his face in his cloak and
went to stand in the mouth of his cave
to hear the voice of God.

John Welch

Tom Bryan

FISH FARM ALBA

The owners are mostly English and scientific,
reliable and sombre, tall and confident.
They set quotas, identify diseases,
prescribe treatments,
kill fish cleanly.

The workers are mostly Scottish,
keep to the hard slog,
smoke, plot, and smoke,
keep a low, subversive profile.

The fish (like me) are neither,
just willing slaves
who fear the freedom beyond tank and cage.
The ancient salmon of wisdom, lobotomised.
(Escaped fish and released fish
swim back forlornly to their nets.)

Some workers hate the fish,
feel the weight of their swimming profits.
Others envy them, would grow fins if they could,
and swim down deep, nothing to lose.

Housing, food and medical treatment thus assured,
until the priest delivers the final head-blow,
which, the experts tell us, is painless.

HERON JACK

Has said nothing to no man since day one,
smokes roll-ups alone, out in the yard.
Takes his teabreak out in the snow,
works shirtless in the scorching sun.

He works like only a maniac can,
with his head down tight, in a hermit's dream.
A bony man, long-legged, sombre, gaunt,
looks like a heron, a heron-man.

But I've seen him watch these birds until
they vanish over the moonscape rock,
then he downs tools, work and food
and stares their flight over the bracken hill.

He then works slowly, without a word,
nods and smiles while the memory fades,
then his thoughts grow dark like the heron's night,
then his dreams plummet down like a stricken bird.

HOLY GROUND

Razor grass bled our trail
to the bluff ridge,
and from thorn jungles there,
we sought the quenching breeze.
Turning north and north again,
like forest pygmies,
we spied on air-conditioned homes
which never shimmered to the heat's command.

Child, bird, stone and tree
flung Pawnee curses
at these heaps of mortar, brick and sand.
We made treaty with bark and earth
on this God-ground,
consecrated by the Sparrow Hawk People.

And we hushed over bones and flint,
on this ravaged mecca of dead Shawnee.
Absorbed the "learning to die" ritual
called "Going to the Sun".

We left our childhoods on that blood-barren clay.
Thirty years later, less strong, less brave,
I could not dare that path today.

CHEROKEE JOHNNY

Cherokee Johnny down our street
had both thumbs gone
and belched from a ponderous belly
which strained beneath the imprint
of a turquoise belt buckle.

Drunk or sober, he slobbered down paths
too sinister for pity,
lurching his body in a tribal chant blues.
Shirtless, under neon and winter moon,
he dragged his dignity like a ball and chain.

JOHN ANGUS

His slow treacle eyes
are pools of wisdom at the world's end.
Witch doctor, medicine man, shadow hunter.
His raven vision misses nothing:
beyond the rotting village hall
he watches ponies grazing
whose owners come from Surrey and Sussex.
His old school is a tea room.

His grandfather's croft is an art gallery.
Too proud to be bitter,
he shares out his Gaelic
with any who will listen.

I watch how his chimney
rises higher than the rest,
and though it is crumbling,
its vibrant smoke rises high enough
to grapple with eagles.

CHARR

Red fish,
like me, tundra-born.
Cold-blooded northerner,
imprisoned and lake-bound
by the Last Ice Age.

A magic name and flesh,
speared by Siberian shaman,
netted by the Cree and Assiniboine.
Sought in deep gorges by the Gael
who called him "tar-dearg" - red belly.
Hunted by entire villages at Martinmas.

He shoals far down and deep,
in Scotland, the last of a dying race.
and so deeply he dwells
that none may know of his final going . . .

Tom Bryan

Illustration to 'Ghost Dances' by Caroline Hunter

Ghost Dances
Donald S Murray

"Why did we come here?" Charlotte complained the day the last of her children left home. "There is nothing to keep people ... Nothing ... Only a stony land and a dangerous ocean."

Farquhar did not answer, surprised by the bitterness of her words. He had always been aware that hidden behind her calm acceptance of life on the island, his wife was deeply unhappy. One of a number of North American Indian women brought back from Canada in the 'twenties, she had for years appeared reconciled to the changes the move caused in her life. After her youngest son followed her other children to the mainland, however, her display of contentment ended. She began to mutter resentfully about her surroundings; its winds, the bare, treeless landscape, the sun that rarely came to light up the skies all became the subjects of her anger. Soon it raged, too, against the native islanders, her sallow skin chilled and white with fury.

"I hate those churchfolk here," she would say. "There is nothing! No colour or music in their lives!"

Farquhar would not disagree with this. He was not a religious man nor did he come from a religious family. His grandfather had been one of the few men who held onto their fiddles when the Church ordered the burning of all the musical instruments on the island. Later, he would entertain his young grandson with stories of former times, describing the movements of the old dances that people once performed on the island - dances that went under queer titles like "The Black Sluggard" and "The Old Woman of the Quern Dust".

"In the Quern Dust dance," he could recall the old man telling him, "the man used to have a piece of wood in his hand which he would wave at the woman, striking not far away from her head as they danced round each other, changing places again and again."

But for all Farquhar's dislike of the church, the vehemence of Charlotte's hatred alarmed him. It seemed to grow as the months went on, a madness that would flame in the darkness of her eyes. There was one time when she met the minister on his walk through the village, greeting the arrival of his black-suited form by spitting on the road. Farquhar mumbled an apology for her actions, more distressed than the minister by her odd behaviour.

"What did you do that for?" he hissed.

Her face became clenched in anger. "They have done more than that to me," she said.

His nervousness in her company increased the day she came back from the well, swinging a half-empty pail of water in her hand. As she stepped into their home, he acknowledged her with a nod, but she seemed not to notice him. It was as if his features - his head with its thick covering of grey hair - were no longer familiar to her. Gesturing to the pail, he spoke: "Why didn't you fill it?"

She didn't even glance at him in reply, but as she placed the pail on the table, he realised she was talking to herself. Her words were neither Gaelic or English, both languages she had learned. No ... At first, he thought her speech was nonsensical - a medley of noises without meaning - but soon he began to realise she was speaking in the Indian language she had used as a child. Startled by the strangeness of her tongue, he rose from his chair.

"What are you saying . . . ?"

There was no response; only her eyes staring, her lips a blur of sounds. A rush of panic passed through him, his voice becoming harsh and sharp.

"Charlotte! Stop it! Stop it!"

Her head jerked back as if she had been stung. Raising her hand to her mouth, she rubbed her lip as if this had been the source of the pain. Tearful, she spoke to him again, this time in English. "I'm sorry," she said. "I forgot."

She walked away, her head low and troubled. He looked after her sadly, convinced that this woman he had loved and taken from the shores of Canada was now losing her mind . . .

A short time after this Farquhar realised why Charlotte behaved in the way she did. He remembered a talk they once had in the early years of their marriage. He had told her that when his people went to school, they were punished for speaking Gaelic by having a wooden collar fixed around their necks. Only English was allowed in the classroom. She nodded with understanding at this, then, hesitantly, went on to tell a story about her own schooldays. If the missionaries who taught them found them speaking any language other than English, their punishment was even more severe. They were made to bite down as hard as they could on a large rubber band. The missionary then stretched this back as far as he could before letting it go - fast and hard - against their mouths. It was in response to this imagined blow that Charlotte had winced, feeling the impact of that rubber band still sore upon her lip some sixty years after the missionary released it from his hand.

Yet there was more to her madness than the memory of past wrongs. There was a longing for her former life; days when she would sit for hours upon the shoreline, as if she hoped to catch a glimpse of, Canada hundreds of miles away. One day she ran the length of their croft to her home, her lined face suddenly fresh and childlike with delight. She dragged out their travelling chest from its place in the bedroom, packing her clothes in a frenzy.

"I'm going!" she shouted. "I'm going home!"

Farquhar wept that night, saddened by the way he had to bring two of the village women to his home to restrain her. As he watched them battle with her, he had seen shades of the Red Indian of legend. Charlotte was whooping and screaming, her fingernails and teeth flashing. The sight had terrified him - the woman whom for years had been close to him transformed into a wild and foreign creature, as unpredictable as the ocean in her moods.

Yet lying beside her in their box-bed, watching her features soften with sleep, he could remember the many times her face had seemed to reflect his own emotions, sharing his pride when she held their first child in her arms, his sorrow when their children had left home - the contrasting events and feelings of a lifetime spent together. Farquhar did not want to lose her. Even though her sanity was ebbing away from her, he did not want to let her go.

Troubled in his sleep, he was still dreaming when she woke him the next morning. The sullen face of the previous night had disappeared and in its place was a new lightness. Her eyes bright with laughter, she poked her head out of the blankets, tickling the tip of his nose with an outstretched finger.

"Wake up, sleepy man," she shouted. "It's time to rise! It's time to shine!"

Nimble as a young girl, she leaped over his side of the bed and began to dress. Her fingers wrestled with her clothing: her arms and legs obstacles to overcome. Finally, she worked her way free, emerging from the snare of a heavy sweater to grin at him. "It's a beautiful day today," she announced.

He nodded, though he could hear the wind and rain roar above the roof-top. The storm rumbled across the chimney, echoing in the room below.

"Do you know what I'm going to do?" she asked. "I'm going to do that dance you told me about. The Ghost Dance! The one Crazy Horse and his followers used to do." She veiled her eyes with her hand, stretching out her arm in a slow, rhythmic manner, chanting as she did so. As suddenly as she began, she stopped, halting her movements abruptly and turning to him for approval. "Let us hope it will bring back the old days, the old ideas just as you hoped it would. Then the buffalo will return to our land, our forests and plains will be restored ... Even our old songs and stories would be heard once again."

He smiled vacantly at her, wondering whom she thought he might be. Her father? Grandfather? He didn't know. All he could be certain of was that for the first time in months she was acting as if he were in the same room. There was interest in her eyes as she spoke to him - even if her words seemed to be those of a child addressing her father than a husband and wife. He felt an odd comfort in listening to her talk, hoping that some sense of companionship could be salvaged from the years they'd spent together.

"Come on . . ." she said, clutching at his hand. "Watch me . . ."

He followed her outside, watching as she stepped into the wind and rain. She slipped nimbly over a puddle, her bare feet leaving prints on the ground. It was then she began her dance, starting in much the same way she had within her home. Her back towards him, she covered her eyes with her hand. As she moved her arm away, she turned on her heel to face him. At the same time, she began to sing, her voice at war with the fury of the storm.

"Ah - yo - ham, ay - yo - ka - be . . ."

He peered at her - this alarming figure he had married. Her black hair was tangled from the wind and her eyes were wide and crazed. She performed a series of frenzied, jagged movements, her toes pounding the mud, while the storm surged around her, making her sway from side to side. Sometimes she was poised on one foot, sometimes the other; but the chanting continued, bringing the people of the village out from their homes to stare at her.

"Aw - ke - yah, far - ka - say . . . "

As he watched her, he felt a longing for much the same things as his wife - for the world to be restored to all it had been before, when both he and Charlotte had laughed at the antics of their children, worked together side by side, sharing the labour of the field, the peat-bank and the shore ...

"She has returned to being a heathen." Domhnall the elder said, looking at Charlotte when she had been brought indoors again. Wearing a dry set of clothes, she sat in the corner, a few strands of her long black hair sticking to her cheekbones. Her jaw jutting outwards, she fixed her visitors - Domhnall and the minister - with a hard and angry look. They seemed unaware of her hostility, ostensibly there to comfort the husband they sat beside.

"No doubt there was always a danger of that happening," the minister said, swallowing a mouthful of tea. "What's bred in the bone often comes out in the flesh. Our Church has seen that so many times in its work in Africa. For every one saved, there are ten who adhere to their old Gods."

Farquhar stared outwards, barely listening to a word his companions said. He was studying Charlotte again, watching how a shy little smile often played on the corners of her face. Looking at her, he could often glimpse the child she had been years ago - the child she had been once more today. Whom had she imagined him to be earlier? Her father? Her grandfather? Most likely, the latter. He imagined him to be an old white-haired man much like his own, sitting her on his knee while he explained the legends and dances of his people, detailing every move their ancient tribesmen had made . . .

"Why do you think that happens?" the elder interrupted.

The minister sighed, his feet outstretched on the clay floor. "I don't know," he declared. "They claim to be Christians for a few years and then they slide back into their old ways, returning to the gods they left behind. These tribal gods bear no resemblance to the Christian one. They could be the ones whom they feel rule the crops and the seasons. Even their dead ancestors. It is to them that they finally give their loyalty . . ."

Half-hearing this, Farquhar remembered the stories told by his grandfather. He had explained why the people of the area performed the dance they called "The Old Woman of the Quern Dust". It had been a corn-dance; one supposed to guarantee that both the crops and Man himself would be restored the following spring. The Old Woman would be struck down and then be brought back to life a short time later - like the seeds from last year's harvest scattered on the earth the following spring. Farquhar could recall, too, the directions he had been given . . .

"The man used to have a piece of wood in his hand which he would wave at the woman, striking not very far from her head as they danced round each other, changing places again and again . . ."

Slowly, he rose from his chair, the conversation of the two men stilling as he did so. Charlotte smiled as he walked towards her, her friendly, open greeting resembling that of a guileless child. She stretched out her hand towards him and he covered it with his own, marvelling at the way her lined and tired face still retained the freshness of childhood, as if the passing of time had not occurred. Yet he knew, too, that if he did not find some way of reaching her, it would not be long before she would be beyond his grasp - as remote as any stranger from him.

It was then he had an idea. He would teach her how to perform the dances of his own people. She would no longer then retreat into a past that was foreign to him - one that belonged to her and her grandfather. With this in mind, he smiled kindly at her, clutching her hand more firmly.

"Can I teach you some new dances?" he said.

And she grinned eagerly in response, looking at him with a love and affection he had not seen in her eyes since the early days of their marriage. She wrapped her arms around him, hugging him closely to her chest.

"I would love you to do that," she said.

Donald S Murray

Màiri NicGumaraid

LA / DAY

Madainn / Morning

Duais mo laighe thràth	My reward for lying early
Fàilt a chur air dùsgadh	Is to welcome the waking
Eiridh mi a shealltainn	I'll rise to see
Dè tha 'n là a' gealltainn	What the day promises
Feuchainn is faireachdainn	Testing and feeling
Roghainnean 's rabhaidhean	Choices and warnings
Fealla-dhà	Fun
Is frogalachd	And cheer
'S na sgeuran a' gealachadh	As the skies lighten

Feasgar / Afternoon

Daoine trang a' dol mu chuairt	Busy people going about
Cuid air lorg ceann-uidhe	Some seeking a destination
'S cuid nach eil	Some not
Agus cuid a dh'iarradh barrachd	And some would ask for more
Na bheir an là seo dhaibh	Than the day will give them
'S b' fheàrr leam gun toireadh	And I wish it would
Nan dèanadh sin iad sona	If that would make them happy
Ard an là a' tarraing air ais	The height of the day pulls back
Na gathan as gile bh' ann	The whitest of the rays
Fuirich gu faic mi	Wait till I see
A' faic mi barrachd	If I can see more
Nas fheàrr na chunna mi roimhe	Better than I saw before

Fionnaradh / Evening

Ruith ruith dhachaigh	Run run home
Steach do dhorus	Through your door
Dùin is glas an saoghal na d' dhèidh	Shut and lock the world behind you
No tionndaidh sìos gu taobh na fàire	Or turn down to the horizon
A' teicheadh ribeagan an là	To chase the fringes of the day
Measg nan solus meallta	Among the fooling lights
Dè tha feitheamh	What's waiting
Cùl an fhaileis	Behind the shadow
Ach an dòchas coibhneil	But gentle hope

Oidhche

Rùm beag dubh - ach dè bhios ann
Dè a th' ann ach thusa 'chridh'
Thusa chridh'
'S far am bi
Bidh mise
'S dùinidh tu an dorus
Air adhbharan na stri

Buailidh uaireadair a' bhaile
Tro 'n oidhche bhlàth mhall
'S cumaidh suain an dorchadais
Fadachd làrna-mhàireach bhuam

CRANN ANNDRAIS

Dh'èirich mi tràth
Madainn bhrèagha
Madainn bhàn
Chaidh mi air lorg Chrann Anndrais

Null tro na gleanntan
Suas na beanntan
Tarsainn aibhnichean
'S mi sireadh Chrann Anndrais

Thachair mi ri Leòdhasach
Bha luath air a chasan
As an dol-seachad
Thuirt e, "Nach tu tha sean fhasanta"

Thachair mi ri Hearrach
A' gabhail a thìd
Thug e smoc às a phìob
'S thuirt e,
"Aidh, well, an Naomh againn fhìn"

'S bha Sasannach
Ann an Siorrachd Pheairt
A' frithealadh mhart
Thuirt e, "Tha, tha thu ceart

Tha rudeigin dhe sheòrs'
Luib Seoc an Aonaidh
'S cha dèanadh e chùis dhuinn
Nis dhol às aonais

Dh'fheumadh na Sasannaich an-uairsin
Rudeigin eile lorg
A chuireadh iad do Sheoc an Aonaidh"

Night

A wee black room - but what's inside
What but you sweetheart
You sweetheart
And where you'll be
I'll be
And you'll close the door
On the roots of stress

The town timepiece will strike
Through the warm slow night
And the sleep of the dark will keep
Tomorrow's longing for me

THE SALTIRE

I rose early
On a lovely morning
A fair morning
I went to seek the Saltire

Over through the glens
Up the mountains
Across rivers
Looking for the Saltire

I met a Lewisman
Fast on his feet
As he tore past
He said, "Aren't you old-fashioned"

I met a Harrisman
Taking his time
He drew on his pipe
And said,
"Aye, well, our own Saint"

And an Englishman
In Perthshire
Was tending cattle
He said, "Yes, yes, you're right

There's something like that
Connected to the Union Jack
And now it wouldn't do
To have to go without it

The English would then need
To find something else
To put into the Union Jack"

BOBBY SANDS A CHAOCHAIL 5.5.81	BOBBY SANDS WHO DIED 5.5.81
Deichead gun a leughadh	A decade without reading him
A lèirsinn fuireach falaicht' bhuam	His vision stays hidden from me
Mo shaoghal-sa dhìth a bhàrdachd-san	My world is without his poetry
Is èideadh cainnte fhaireachdainn	And the armoured words of his feelings
Mo smuaintean fhathast às aonais	My thoughts are still without
Roinn de na chuir e thairis	A share of what he put across
Na òige, na aithne	In his youth, his knowledge
Na èiginn, na bheatha.	His oppression, his life.
Deichead gun a leughadh	A decade without reading him
A reusan a' sìor-amharc orm	His reason is eternally staring at me
Mo thuigse a' toirt aire dha	My understanding is giving him his place
'S e m' fheum a-nis a leasachadh	My need is now to make it better
Mo dhleasdanas san àm seo	My duty at this time
A bhith gu mòr an urram	Is to greatly honour
Do adhbhar, a chùram	His cause, his care
A bhàs, a bheatha.	His death, his life.

WITH JUST A TOUCH OF TOBERMORY

    I see you claim you're Scottish
    and more
    and before
    I know where I am
    you'll be telling me I'm foreign
    because this is England
    with just a touch of Tobermory

    A littleness of Island
    and Gaelicness of name
    where tourists tap teutonic toes
    and pat their tartaned laps
    tart
    what a lot
    a culture bought and sold

    Is that a dialect I detect
    from here
    oh dear
    you give me cause to weep
    for all the words we never speak
    that lie in print
    embalmed with love and tender grief

    A thirst for vengeance
    don't dare say
    our rhythms now a requiem ring
    to old clandestine dreams
    clan
    what
    surely not
    a people quiet and keen

FRUIT GUMS

A man with a big brown bag
And big brown feet
And airy trousers made of tweed
Hairy and airy
And his hands would be hairy
And maybe his face
If I could remember seeing it

He stuck a needle into me
My mother held me firm across her knees
And tried not to get too bruised
By the kicking
Or too embarrassed by the screaming
That far-off neighbours could listen to
And smile
When it was jagtime again

And the world had a lid on it
That came down as far as my eyebrows
And the big brown man stretched all the way up
Then left
To play his part
In the out-of-sight

The pain goes quickly
But not the hurt
How dare they make my world
A bare-bottomed eyebrow-levelled
Place

Just a moment since
It had colour and light
And me moving in it
And the right kind of noise

But then they'd come
Enough to fit my hand
Pieces of sunshine and fruit
Round here and bumpy there
Sweet and fine and smooth
And friendly

And the whole world returned
And my feet could hold me up
Till I could sit down again

Maybe I always forgot
Not to scream
Or maybe I didn't

Mary Montgomery

Itinerary of a Song:
Cross-Cultural Connections from Scotia to Nova Scotia and Beyond
Colin Nicholson

> Yet it seemed a bad thing to have lost a language... The lost languages forever lurking in the ventricles of the hearts of those who had lost them. (*The Diviners*, Margaret Laurence)

"In my early teens," recalls Sorley MacLean, "that is from about 1924, I realised that I was a traditional Gaelic singer *manqué*, for I was born into a family of tradtional singers and pipers on all sides, and that in a Free Presbyterian community, of all the most inimical to such 'vanities'... I think that the first great 'artistic' impact on me was my father's mother singing some of the very greatest of Gaelic songs, and all in her own tradtional versions." (*Chapman* 16) MacLean explains his inability as a "defect in pitch", adding, "even to this day, I sometimes think that if I had been a singer I would have written no verse." So MacLean's might be described as a displaced art, from the singing voice to the printed page; but his statement is endorsed by Barthes' claim that "a language is constituted in the individual through his learning from the environmental speech." I will focus here on the conjunction of song with environmental speech and its imaginative inscription in Scottish and Scots-Canadian writing, identifying elements in cross-cultural discursive formations associated with the Scottish diaspora in North America.

"All poetry," MacLean wrote in the 1930s, "reflects social phenomena, and in the Highlands of the 19th century emigration of one kind or another was the phenomenon of phenomena... The Highland Clearances constitute one of the saddest tragedies that has ever come upon a people, and one of the most astounding of all the successes of landlord capitalism in Western Europe, such a triumph over the workers and peasants of a country as has rarely been achieved with such ease, cruelty and cynicism." His verse explores traumatising experiences of personal and trans-national kinds. In his elegiac poem for his native Skye, 'The Island', we read:

> Great Island, Island of my desire,
> Island of my heart and wound,
> it is not likely that the strife
> and suffering of Braes will be seen requited...
>
> there is no hope of your townships
> rising high with gladness and laughter,
> and your men are not expected
> when America and France take them.

Maclean has given resonant voice to the agony of deracination and dislocation in memorable lines from 'The Woods of Raasay': they rise "from the miserable torn depths/ that puts their burden on mountains." His poetry raises itself passionately against the erosion of Gaelic society and identity and it has been rightly said that "power which can overwhelm features strongly in MacLean's poetry, as it does in Highland experience." Although there have been significant developments recently concerning school instruction in Gaelic in the Scottish Highlands and Islands, the imposition from 1872 onwards of a compulsory English-only education effected a transforming extension of England's imperialising control over Gaelic territories. So it is a difficult irony that in 1987 the Iona Foundation produced an English-language-only version of MacLean's verse for American readers. Not a little ruefully, Iain Crichton Smith, who writes in both Gaelic and English and who was the first to translate MacLean for a wider audience says of him that he "has achieved much of his reputation by means of his translations, and essays are confidently written about him by those who don't know Gaelic."

But Crichton Smith is more germane to our argument, guilt-stricken as he is that although he did not learn English until age five when he went to school, he now writes more in English than Gaelic. "In school I spoke English in the school, in the playground, and Gaelic at home." He adds, "the very fact that I had to learn English when I was at school was probably registered in some obscure corner of my psyche as an indication that English was superior to Gaelic." Referring to himself as a linguistic "double man", (the title of his essay in *The Literature of Region and Nation*, ed R P Draper) Smith has imaged his predicament in a Gaelic poem called 'The Fool' where a surface simplicity of utterance is complicated by allusive gestures to *King Lear*.

> In the dress of the fool, the two colours that
> have tormented me, English and Gaelic, the
> court of injustice, the reason for my anger, and
> that fine rain from the mountains and these grievous
> storms from my mind streaming the two colours
> together so that I will go with poor sight in the one
> colour that is so odd that the King himself will not
> understand my conversation.

So there is an added poignancy in lines from 'Eight Songs For a New Ceilidh': "I will never go to France, my dear, my dear, though you are young. I am tied to the Highlands. That is where I learned my wound." The wound is historical, as a poem like 'The Clearances' emphasises:

> The thistles climb in the thatch. Forever
> this sharp scale in our poems,
> as also the waste music of the sea.
>
> The stars shine over Sutherland
> in a cold ceilidh of their own,
> as, in the morning, the silver cane
>
> Cropped among corn. We will remember this.

But these cross-cultural pressures and determinations also register in distinctly existential, and continuing, ways: "It is bitter/ to be an exile in one's own land./ It is bitter/ to walk among strangers/ when the strangers are in one's own land./ It is bitter/ to dip a pen in continuous water/ to write poems of exile/ in a verse without honour or style." The other side of that coin - and the dead metaphor stirs discomfitingly - is expressed in a poem called 'The Exiles', originally written in Gaelic:

> The many ships that left our country
> with white wings for Canada.
> They are like handkerchiefs in our memories
> and the brine like tears
> and in their masts sailors singing
> like birds on branches.

His own translation of a poem called 'Shall Gaelic Die?' explores the problem and develops the image of the fool's motley: "When the Higlands loses its language, will there be a Highlands,/ said I, with my two coats, losing, perhaps, the two." The poem asks, with edgy irony, "In what language would you say, "Fhuar a' Ghaidhlig bas?'" ("Gaelic is dead").

Across the body of his writing, Crichton Smith inscribes a Highland sensibility, registering a distinctive and often Gaelic purpose and place for the English-speaking world. Again, his alertness to the historical and geographical extension of Scottish relationship and identity to North America comes to us in dimensions that are both personal, immediate and celebratory, and also historical, in more elegaic vein. His recent long poem 'My Canadian Uncle' records a visit to his 85-year-old uncle Torquil, then living in Vancouver, who had left Lewis for Canada in a cattle ship in 1912. It is an entertaining poem for several reasons, not least a form which moves through rhyme and para-rhyme to free verse and back as Scottish and Canadian elements are recapitulated. Warming to his uncle's conversation and experiences, Crichton Smith travels back in his mind to the historical memory of the depopulation of Gaelic territories:

> From superficial Canada I saw
> the white ship swelling with her ruinous sails.
> The emigrants are dressed in their new suits.
> Handkerchiefs wave from the pier and from the boats.
> Someone begins a psalm, and the music floats
> eerily between the Atlantic and the shore.
> Someone is slamming a big salty door.
> From the sharp-scaled pier the scales rise, sharp and pure.
>
> This is their drama and their literature.
> The island's bare but for the few sparse trees
> around the Castle. There's a cold sharp breeze
> drifts between the mother and the son.
> To him it's an adventure, to her, ruin.
> The ship begins to move. The voices fade.
> Sometimes by masts at moonlight they'll hear the dead
> voices crying over the wrinkled graves.

'My Canadian Uncle' signifies a resurrection of those transatlantic voices, a celebration of Scots-Canadian cadence and idiom. Elegaic in mode, the poem turns classically at its close to speak to living continuities: "I prefer/ to think of him telling stories in his house,/ huge, craggy, confident, while that velvet rose/ glowed in the garden below squawking crows."

The stories which Nova Scotia writer Alistair MacLeod tells also figure departures and returns. They too register narrative concerns with Highland origination, and are equally imbued with an awareness of "the significance of ancestral islands" even though for some of his characters they are "long left and never seen." These memories, though, are counteracted and edged towards immediate Nova Scotian continuities by MacLeod's prevalent option for a present-tense, first-person narrative. A Canadian 'now' surfaces through a Scottish 'then'. Conjuring intertextual echoes of Crichton Smith's "cold sharp breeze ... between the mother and the son", the narrator of MacLeod's award-winning story 'The Boat' (*The Lost Salt Gift of Blood*, Toronto 1967), who has left maritime small-boat fishing to teach at "a great Mid-western university", reflects "it is not an easy thing to know that your mother looks upon the sea with love and on you with bitterness because the one has been so constant and the other so untrue." MacLeod belongs to the first generation of Nova Scotians for whom the breakdown of Gaelic culture is beginning to occur, and 'The Boat' composes a meditation upon the inexorable breaking of "links in the chain of tradition." When the narrator recalls hearing for the first time his father singing "the wild and haunting Gaelic war songs of those spattered Highlanders he had never seen" he goes on to remember that "when his voice ceased, the savage melancholy of three hundred years seemed to hang over the peaceful harbour."

Again as if in scripted response to Crichton Smith's voiced unease, Alistair MacLeod habitually incorporates Gaelic phrase and saying into his English-language medium, enshrining them for memory even as he signifies their linguistic transformation into the contours of an anglophone Canadian textuality. "The transition from Gaelic to English that is regularly noted in these stories, and that is marked also by the need to gloss the few still-surviving Gaelic expressions . . . constitutes one of the most significant displacements out of which MacLeod forges his fiction." (Arnold E. Davidson, 'As Birds Bring Forth the Story', *Canadian Literature* 119)

As past gives way to present in these stories, one repeated device which provides genealogical immediacy for historic resonance, assuming symbolic significance, is the figure of the dying father or grandfather, or of the ageing male. The opening story in *As Birds Bring Forth The Sun* (Toronto, 1986), marks a further moment of slippage as the narrator, a miner called Mackinnon, realises that the Gaelic miners' chorus he leads is becoming "as lonely and irrelevant as it was meaningless." They become parodies of themselves, "standing in rows, wearing our miner's gear ... to mouth our songs to batteries of tape recorders and to people who did not understand them." This is further developed in the ironically-titled 'The Tuning of Perfection' where a 78-year-old descendant of a great-grandfather referred to as "the man from Skye" has, since his recent discovery by the folklorists, "come to be regarded as 'the last of the authentic old-time Gaelic Singers'". The old man refuses to compromise the purity of his art for the sake of a televised "Scots Around the World" celebration to be beamed across Canada. The competition is won, instead, by a neighbouring family who sing "a bunch of nonsense syllables strung together" to an unknowing audience.

Boundaries are further extended in short fiction which registers uncertainties in a manner not unlike MacLeod's in the stories gathered together for D R MacDonald's first collection, *Eyestone* (New York. 1987).

Iterative configurations associated with the Scottish diaspora receive echo and sometimes uneasy endorsement. Patterns of death and dying, of displacement and return, of familial and historic memory, of possession of and alienation from senses of territorial place, of Gaelic phrase and saying recorded and translated and of the structure of syntax to convey distinctive Nova Scotian cadence and rhythms of speech are inscribed to similar yet different effect. And one of the differences is that American intrusions now form part of the pattern of return. The narrator of 'The Chinese Rifle', having moved from Cape Breton to Ohio as a child, has returned to settle the estate after the death of his parents - property values, and knowledge of corporate capitalism in the market-place come to prominence at times in this writing - and we read: "but in this town we were extinguished. Nothing of us would remain with this place but two small, almost anonymous gravestones that would go unvisited in a burial park where no flowers were allowed."

International conflict (two World Wars, Korea and Vietnam), surface in the narration, and the rifle which names the story is a trophy from one of them. In the service of a New York-based but internationally-trading publishing company for which he devises and edits texts for teaching English as a second language, our narrator has the feeling that he wants "to hold something together even though I was no longer sure what it was."

In the preceding story, Graham Chisholm also left Cape Breton for the USA as a young man, "moving slowly and vaguely westward until he reached California, already ten years from home," and has returned for the burial of a brother who had stayed. "They did not hold the old-time wakes any more, just a remnant of them, an evening of visitors at the funeral home. No more all-night vigils. And where in New Skye would you go now for a fiddler, and enough dancers to fill this room?" Drinking moonshine liquor with locals on the wharf, the conversation turns to the only eligible girl in New Skye, who has been practising the bagpipes for a forthcoming Gaelic Mod.

"You men going to the Mod?"
"Jesus, half the pipers are Yanks!" Kenny said.
"Oh, we'll go over one night or other," Rob said.
"Might find a couple of girls among the tourists and throw a little Gaelic at them. Some go for that."
It's damn little I'll be throwing at them," Kenny said.

MacDonald's great-grandfather emigrated from Gairloch to Boularderie Island, Cape Breton, in the early 1800s, and his grandfather could read and write Gaelic as well as English. Though born in Cape Breton, MacDonald moved to Ohio as a child and grew up there. Like the narrator of MacLeod's 'The Boat', MacDonald is a university lecturer, but in Stanford, California. Two biographical facts are relevant here, and the first connects with Crichton Smith's remarks about his half-hidden awareness that learning English at school lent it an aura of superiority. "Although my grandparents," MacDonald remembers, "on both sides were fluent Gaelic speakers, neither my mother nor father carried the language into adulthood... English was the tongue of the world at large, and even in the 1900s Cape Bretoners were going south to Boston to escape the depressed economy of their own region."

The main character of 'Eyestone', MacDonald's title story, is Royce. His surname calculatedly withheld. He is an artist who has given up teaching college in Boston and bought a farm in Cape Breton from an old Gaelic-speaking couple, the Corbetts, to set up an artists' colony there with his wife. Ohe plans fail and his wife goes back to Boston. The bargain struck with the Corbetts was that they be allowed to live out their lives in the farmhouse. Having extracted this promise, old Mr Corbett, suffering ill-health for some time, hanged himself in the barn. That was a year before the opening of the story, and these things pass through Royce's mind as he potters disconsolately around his property. Senses of ontological insecurity are triggered, with his developing uneasiness over the continuing presence of Mrs Corbett. "How was it she could make him feel like a trespasser?" Not only that, but as he "glimpses" her in the woods she seems to have the ability to appear and vanish at will; "suddenly she is there, and then not."

Not seeing yet the nature of his responsibilities to the old lady, Royce has already wondered, in free-floating discourse which drifts in and out of his focalising consciousness, dissolving other boundaries, "Is it callous to think she might die to oblige him?" Gathering senses of guilt are compounded when we read, "the day Royce brought the papers round for (old Corbett) to sign, Mrs Corbett, whispering to herself in Gaelic, sat glumly in one corner of the parlor as if her husband were selling not the land but her." Although Royce has purchased the place, he has little purchase upon it. "He pokes around the barn touching things he owns but that never seem his." Separated as he is from his wife, Royce's displacement is both geographical and emotional and constitutes a condition of alienation classically conceived and rendered in appropriately artistic metaphor. "When Royce is inside the barn, his careful, exact drawings seem to have no connection at all to it. The sharp warmth, the worn surfaces have an intimacy he longs to feel on canvas but cannot."

Varying a technique employed by MacLeod, MacDonald uses an imagery of vanishing traces to convey Royce's feelings of rootless transience: "dense grass he stomped down is combed back by the wind as if he never passed there", or to suggest his inability properly to construe either Mrs Corbett or his relationship to her. "Often he has come across her trail, sometimes no more than a faint cleavage through fern, a cloudy footprint in brookside mud. When he looks up again, she is gone." But the pervasive ocular and perceptual imagery concentrates when a held branch slips and strikes Royce in the face, leaving "a bit of needle or bark" under his eyelid, which scratches at his eyeball, causing him acute discomfort, and his eye to weep copiously, further blurring his already dubious perception. Mrs Corbett's sureness of touch in the woods contrasts with Royce's carelessness. Earlier he has seen her among the trees, "working her hand over the trunks of a fir, stroking its bark for pitch" If she is aware of him, she gives no sign. She is singing in a soft cooing rill a Gaelic song he has heard her sing before. *"Tha mo chul ruit, Tha mo chul ruit..."* Is it some charm for gathering balsam, for urging sap from the tree?

Finally he discovers the significance of the Gaelic. "What words are they?" he asks her. She had sensed him in the woods all along. "They say 'My back to you, My back to you . . . You're not of my kin.' It's only a song that pigeons sing. The birds knew Gaelic once." Before that, his injured eye filling with water, Royce has told her she must quit the house so that he might occupy it and tempt his wife to rejoin him. Mrs Corbett receives the news calmly. That evening Royce contemplates "the colour and light above the shoreline trees... he used to sketch in pastel." But now he no longer bothers. "Even his good eye is getting sore from the strain. And evicting the old lady bothers him."

The word triggers a set of historical associations to provide resonant context for Royce's subsequent brooding and his dawning realisation:

> And now he owns this land. Does he not? He has not stolen it. Didn't they let so much of their land slip away, these people, let it go to so many strangers like himself that even the government got alarmed?...
> Not Mrs Corbett. He raises his glass to her, and drinks.

Royce's projected eviction makes him a contemporary representative of that landlord capitalism excoriated by Sorley MacLean. But here the narrative turns. Rather the worse for rum, Royce visits Mrs Corbett. "'It's for your eye you're here,' she says,". He offers to paint her portrait and she declines. "'Oh, there'll be no pictures of me, and this is no kind of light for doing them.' He cannot see her face clearly, as he had not that afternoon Corbett signed over the land." But Mrs Corbett, the seventh daughter of a seventh son and so the carrier of legendary powers, places the eyestone "like a tiny white pebble," under his eyelid. "Listen Mrs Corbett," says Royce, "you don't have to leave the house. Stay. Stay as long as you like." "I have done that," is her reply.

The eyestone brings him relief. As if in compensation, the narrative environment produces an answerable discourse. The rain is sings over the windows, and "the wind coos in the stove flue." Royce's surname is uttered for the first time when the old lady announces, "Royce Simmons, the house is yours," and then she vanishes from the text. When he calls after her, "his voice drifted into the recesses of the house." The moment signifies a different kind of territorial possession, imaginatively achieved, seemingly vatic and oracular but somehow emerging naturalistically.

In tales much concerned with permanence and passing, with Highland origins and folk-memory and their Nova Scotian transmutations, the 'American' MacDonald traces roots and rootlessness in suggestive ways, and forges a distinctive voice in the process. "I am not done," he says, "writing fiction that comes, from one direction or another, out of Cape Breton, or perhaps I should say that Cape Breton is not done with me." That is good to hear, and since they speak directly to several of the concerns we have been outlining, the narrator's words which close MacDonald's volume signal a convenient stopping-place:

> I do not understand the heavens or their arrangements as they move through the seasons of the skies. Put my father on a dark and empty sea and still he will not be lost. I think he has never been lost. I must memorise the constellations, learn to guide myself through these winter nights. I stare into the vortex the ivy makes and imagine that black hole my father will wither into, gone beyond the skies that helped him, hindered him. All I know for certain, is that we are sailing.

Colin Nicholson

Gordon Meade

THE YEAR OF THE ECLIPSE

Everyday was winter,
Though the sun shone through the ward's
Blank windows, and at night, the radiators
Kept us warm. A row of potato-heads,
Planted in identical beds, two pillows,
Two sheets, two blankets, one spread.

Every so often, one
Of us would escape, either out, or down.
Along the waxed corridors to a new freedom,
Or another 'Home'. Our numbers never
Changed, replacements coming in one by one.
A new face, a new name, another

Number in the game.
Spring came with me ready to bloom,
To burst out of the white-sheeted earth,
Unfurl my leaves, and flower. A shower
Of words rained upon my bulbed head. My
Eager feelers drank them all in.

I felt I was ready
To be transplanted into a bed of my
Own. Ready to grow in a garden I could
Call my home. Summer may have been
Too hot, but housed behind the glass of
A cold-frame, I was never warm. Only

The blood-clots felt
The heat of the sun. Crinkled, they
Flaked off and fell, like bombs, onto
The ripped tarpaulin of my brain.
The clock ticked slowly through the long
Afternoons, the sleepless, sweaty

Evenings. And if I did
Sleep, I'd dream of a pock-marked moon,
And not a healing sun. Autumn ended it.
A drift of leaves buffeted against
My door, and I woke under a floor carpeted
With wrinkled faces. In my mind,

A legless man in a high-
Rise flat was dying, and in the room
Above, the mattress smelt of the stained
Sheets of the incontinent dead,
Their last wishes dripping onto my raw
Head. I woke up, washed, and

Dressed. Got ready to
Face another winter in another ward.
The sea was far away, and all the birds
Had flown. I woke up talking,
As I had done in my sleep all along.
I woke up talking, about the sun.

ARCTURUS

Underneath the crest of Arcturus, one
of the trawlers in Eyemouth's fishing fleet,
are written the words - Hazard Yet Forward.

Arcturus, the bear-ward,
Sits at her table of water and waits
For her people to join her, to drift
Towards her from quayside bars.

She's painted in the blue of heaven,
Yet her flags are the darkness of night.
Her lights flare red and green for
Hazard, for progress, white.

We hear that her namesake is
A yellow star in Boötes, the fourth in order
Of brightness in the entire universe.
We hear also, that the bear is sacred

To the moon, and that the Great
And Little Bears are the hands of the Goddess.
We watch Arcturus slide out of the harbour
And disappear from sight. Beneath

The moon, she floats above
A shoal of silver darlings, dependant for
Her safety on the hands of her captain,
And the mercy of the ocean's might.

INDIAN TALK

I remember a young boy's back broken.
I remember a young boy's skull smashed.
I remember a young boy's hip kicked out
of joint and healing in the wrong place.
I remember a young girl hit in the mouth
with a leather strap for talking Indian
in class. And I remember at night in bed
recreating all the conversations I'd ever
had just to keep our language alive.

WHALE HOTEL

Drinking in the Whale,
We are whalers after a fashion, both
Hunting with words. We fling them, like darts,
At the targets of imagination.

We spear our subjects -
Mine, a shell scoured clean, and yours,
A piece of fruit, as luscious to the ear as
A dream of freedom to a prisoner

Of fear. Inside the Whale,
We pass the afternoons - pressganged
Members of a crew still waiting for its instructions,
Still searching for a hint, a glimpse

Of destination. We leave
In ships of steel across a sea without
Dimension. We sail in opposite, though not
Opposed, directions - mine, towards

A beach littered with wrecks
Of death's invention, and yours, towards
An island orchard, bearing apples grown on
Boughs of love's intention.

Gordon Meade

A Sort of Love Story
Pete Fortune

*Gin a body kiss a body
need the warld ken?* - Robert Burns

I lift the receiver and dial her number and it seems to ring ring ring forever. I'm just about to give up on her when at last she's there.

"Hello," (let's call her D). Never a name, never a number, just a hello.

"Hello," I say. "I was just about to give up on you. Is it okay to talk?"

She sounds flustered. "I suppose so. Eh, look, I don't know. Maybe it's not. I mean, is it okay to talk?"

"What's wrong?" I ask.

"Well, is it okay?" she asks. "I've been doing some thinking." She goes quiet and I'm about to speak, but then she starts up again. "What are we supposed to be doing? I mean, why do you phone me nearly every day?"

I know what she's getting at but find myself playing dumb. "I've been having a rough day at work and decided what I needed was a friendly voice to cheer me up, but, you know, so far it's not working out too well."

"If you're needing cheering up, why don't you phone your wife?"

"She's at work," I tell her. Then I say, "You're making me confused here. What are you getting at?"

"What am I getting at? We've been meeting for a couple of months now and you phone me nearly every day and you ask what I'm getting at? What am I supposed to make of all this?"

"Hey, come on." I've got the fake-hurt voice on now. "We're just friends and, well, it's not as if there's anything going on, is there?"

"Does your wife know we meet and that you phone so often?"

"No, of course not. Does George? Is that what's wrong?"

"No, George doesn't know a thing. Look, it's just that . . . well, what we're into here isn't really normal, is it? I mean . . ."

I interrupt her. "Oh come on. What *is* normal? Look, we're just friends."

Still she goes on. "Look, I'm sorry but we're going to have to think things through. Maybe we are just friends, but for how long? And if we are just friends, why the need for all the underhand stuff? Tell you what - next time we go out together, tell your wife. Tell her you're going out with another woman but that she's not to worry. Tell her we're just friends.

". . . You still there? You listening?"

"I'm listening," I tell her, "just let me light a cigarette." My left eyelid is twitching. Whenever I'm nervous about something it starts twitching and right now it's jumping like mad. "Okay," I tell her, "if we're not just friends, what are we? What is all this? Why the sudden need for ground rules - is that what you want? Some sort of Constitution?"

Silence. Then she speaks and her voice is softer and calmer. "Look, maybe it's just me, but somehow I don't think so." Silence again, and I feel a bit wobbly and tremble a little as I play with my cigarette packet. "Will you stop sparring with me?" she says.

"We're just friends," I say, and I laugh a little because I haven't a clue what else to do. I'm about to say something - *anything* - when she gives me this:

"If I keep seeing you then I'm scared I'm going to end up in deep. That's the God's honest truth. I don't know how you feel, but that's my position. I don't think I want that to happen but I don't know what I want, right? Don't phone tomorrow, leave off for a bit. I'll see you at the end of the week, I'll see you on Friday. You tell me on Friday where we go from here, okay?"

"That's not fair," I protest, but off she goes again.

"What we're doing isn't fair - at least it's not fair on some people is it? Look, this isn't easy, I should have written. Tell me on Friday where we go from here, you listening? Tell me to get lost if you want to - just tell me something for God's sake."

"Hold on," I say. She's ranting a bit now and what I can't handle is this taking place here, at work. (I'm later phoning today and my boss Farquharson is due back in the office any time). "Maybe we should meet. I can make an excuse and meet you some place. How does that sound?"

"Friday," she says. "You have to think about things and tell me on Friday."

And then she's off. The phone goes dead and I put the receiver back where it belongs. I slump back into my chair and the first thing I focus on is the picture of my boys I have pinned to the wall. I pick up the phone and stab at the buttons. "Friday," she says, "leave it till Friday." She sounds like she could be crying.

I'm elated and terrified all at once. I write the word 'adultery' on my doodle pad and underline it, then score through it until it can't be read. I write 'LOVE' in capital letters and place a question mark to the left and right of it, then tear the sheet off and throw it in my waste bin. Picking up a little vanity mirror I keep nearby I see my very ordinary face. Across this very ordinary forehead seems to be written *married man*, but my beard and moustache look neat. My beard and moustache are neatly trimmed and my wife has commented on this. She mentions too that I dress smarter than I used to and sometimes jokes around that maybe I have a blonde hidden away somewhere.

Maybe I do.

I scribble a note for Farquharson saying I'm sorry but something's cropped up at home and I'll call him later. I can't stay here - I'm heading for some bar or other, only because I can think of nowhere else to go. I take the crumpled-up doodle-pad page from the waste bin and put it in my jacket pocket. I check my wallet and leave. Before I do, I look at the photo of my boys again. Jake and Harry. Jake nine years old, Harry six in a couple of weeks. In that photo they look like they're good boys and they look like they're happy boys.

Everybody says so.

In the pub I buy a beer and a large whisky and sit with a *Guardian* folded to the crossword page, hoping this will be enough to deter any day-time drunks looking for someone to trade blethers with. The beer tastes metallic but the whisky is good. I push the beer to the side and finish my whisky then buy another. I light a cigarette and study the matchbox. This brand is called *Bright Sparks* and on the reverse they run a series of (what they call) smartass one-liners. My one says *Beware of all Enterprises that require New Clothes*. I underline it. Underlining things is a habit of mine but sitting in bars thinking of women when I should be working definitely isn't.

Know what? Lots of people I know have had marriages fall apart on them. Why do they get involved in *that* game? I say to my wife. All these people chasing a bit of the extra-marital and look where it gets them. (Lust always gets the blame: nobody mentions love.) I say this to Ann some evenings when I'm mellow with whisky and hoping that she doesn't have a headache.

I need fresh air and so decide to walk home. I take the long route, which means cutting through the grave-yard and climbing a dry-stane dyke into fields and then up into the hills. I come here often. I come here to take the clean air and marvel at the sweeping panorama of the town and the surrounding lush green hills. Sometimes D and I walk here and talk and laugh a lot and it makes me feel as if I'm a teenager again.

How does *that* feel?

It feels like everything is fresh and exciting, and it's about wandering around in a sort of limbo when I'm not with her. It's about trying to visualise her face and her hair and recalling snippets of conversation and all the time looking for clues.

Who needs clues now?

I think now of her smile and the way she throws back her head and laughs her big happy laugh, then covers her mouth with her hand as if somehow she shouldn't be laughing like that at her age. Only last week D and I were joking about getting old and she said we could put all this down to a mid-life crisis. I wanted to say "put *what* down to a mid-life crisis?" but I didn't. God knows I wanted to, but I didn't.

There's a good breeze blowing and it's making a gentle swishing sound through the trees, but all the same I am really warm and have to take my jacket off. I fold it over my arm but my wallet and cigarettes fall out so I have to fill my trouser pockets to bulging. I still have the piece of crumpled doodle-pad and I flatten it out and look at the word LOVE snuggled in between the question marks. High above me I catch the glint of a plane and maybe just the drone of its engine. I think of all those people up there and wonder where they are heading.

And down here there's me and my crumpled doodle-pad, me slightly drunk on whisky and country smells and God knows what else. I fold the doodle page into a paper dart and launch it into a flight as smooth as that plane up above. It floats up, then dips down out of sight behind a gorse bush, and I get to thinking how Jake and Harry would have enjoyed seeing that.

From somewhere the sound of cattle. Suddenly I'm cold again so I put my jacket back on and head for home. Home is where the heart is. (Where's that?) Despite wearing a suit I decide to continue along the top of the hills and scramble over some crags, and make for home that way. Once, near the spot where I'm at now, D took my hand and kissed me lightly on the cheek, and dear God it sent an electric shock through me. Listen to this stuff - from married old *me*. I didn't ask for this, and I certainly didn't go looking for it. (Somewhere along the way life ambushed me.) But I have it - I have this sort-of-relationship with another woman and I'm not too sure what it means.

Maybe I thought things could just carry on the way they were, but it seems not. 'In deep,' she said. Maybe me too (not waving but drowning?).

My suit is in reasonable nick when I arrive home, but my shoes are a tapestry of mud and all sorts of grime. I discard them in the garage, then go upstairs and phone work. I leave a message for Farquharson explaining that I don't feel so well but should be back in tomorrow.

My wife comes home to find me sat at the breakfast bar, supping a lager.

"Why are you home?" she asks. "Are you not well?"

"Could be better," I tell her, "but nothing to worry about."

"Can't be, not if you can sit here and drink beer. What's up?"

"Nothing, Ann. I'm okay." I don't feel like talking.

"How long have you been here? You could at least have collected the boys from Mary."

"Sorry," I tell her, "it didn't occur to me."

"It didn't occur? You're sat here drinking beer when you say you don't feel well and your boys don't *occur* to you?"

She goes off in a kind of huff to collect the boys and I'm glad to be left alone. I go out the back to take some fresh air and slightly drunk I perch myself in front of the rabbit hutch and say hello to Snowy. He stares impassively back. Sometimes on our strolls we see rabbits scurrying about the fields and I tell D about Snowy and how bad I sometimes feel at him being cooped up all the time. I tell her how good it would be if he could romp about like that, but he's been cooped up so long he wouldn't manage for himself out there in the big bad world. He might be bored, but he's safe. D laughs and tells me I'm a soppy old fool and I laugh along with her and tell her she doesn't know just how right she is.

I run upstairs and phone Farquharson.

"How are you?" he asks.

"Fine," I tell him, "just listen. Meet me tonight. I'll see you around eight in the Star. Can you manage that?"

"I don't know. Liz might have things planned. I thought you were ill? You sound sort of frantic."

"Be there please. It's important. Say you'll be there - I'll explain later."

Ann arrives back with the boys and I tell her I'm sorry about my acting strangely, but that Farquharson and I have the chance of a big one at work and that we have to meet later to work things out. I tell her it's preying on my mind. She wants to know more but I tell her to wait until later. I cook dinner and reflect on how easy it is these days to tell lies. How come something so special is making me into something so bad?

We are the sum total of our past. Farquharson is fond of coming out with stuff like that, but it's not so much the past I'm concerned with right now.

Good old Farq. One New Year he got uncharacteristically drunk and confided in me about a fling he'd had with a neighbour's wife. Pure lust, he'd said, and his mouth made a sort of smacking sound when he'd said that. Lust. Dangerous game though, he'd said, not to be recommended; and with all that booze flowing through him he'd become mildly hectoring, old Farq playing the role of mentor. I reckon Farq owes me one.

I do more than my usual share of cleaning up after dinner then go upstairs to run a bath for the boys. I feel jaded and find myself stripping off and climbing into the bath. Let the boys play out a little longer I tell my wife. It's a really fine night, I tell her. They can have the water after me.

The bath is bliss and I allow my eyes to close, then get to thinking about the situation I'm in. I love Ann and my boys, but I want D too. (I want my head looking into.) Jake comes into the bathroom to take a pee and he tells me he's had enough playing outside in the garden and that he wants to have a bath. "Can I have a bath with you Dad?" he wants to know, and then will I read him a story? I tell him I'm sorry but I have to go and meet Farq because we have things to talk about.

"What do you have to talk about, Dad? Is it important?"

He has me reeling here and before I know it I start blabbering like a baby. My boy has never seen me crying before and off he goes bawling for his mum. Ann comes in and she's looking really concerned, and the boys are hovering behind her looking puzzled and frightened. I have such a sore stomach, I tell them. You go out and play and let me tell Mum about it. Harry buys this but Jake is no fool and we have a job getting him to go back outside. But he goes. He goes outside and I'm left with the realisation that I'm about to give him his first taste of the adult world. (This is what it means to be grown-up, son - stay nine years old for as long as you can.)

And then I tell Ann the lot. I tell her I've become friendly with this woman and that without realising what was happening have become really attached to her. I mean *really* attached to her. She is a queer mixture of sadness and anger. I won't tell her who it is, no, she doesn't know her, no, we haven't slept together, and yes, she is married too. I can scarcely believe I am saying all these things but know that it is too late now even to contemplate the 'Ha ha, had you fooled then!' line.

There are drawers being opened and closed and I hear the suitcase being dragged down from the top of our wardrobe. (We have two wardrobes but always liked the idea of our clothes being in there together.) She looks back into the bathroom and says "Do you love each other?"

I tell her I don't know and ask if she'll please put that suitcase away. She tells me she thinks it best if she goes away for a few days. She says we both have some thinking to do, and it's better we do it apart. She's told the boys she's tired and needs a break and is going to see her parents for a few days.

Jake comes back into the bathroom. I expect him to be asking loads of questions but he's really quiet and just looking at me. He just keeps looking at me and I give him a hug and ask him if he's going with his mum, or does he want to stay here with me. "I'll go with Mum," he says. Then he looks me in the eye and asks, "Do you mind?"

I'm standing in the driveway and they are in the car and I'm waving goodbye. There has been no screaming or bawling or fighting, but she is going. A wave seems a ludicrous response. Ann reverses the car down the drive, she reverses down the drive too quickly and she sort of skids and throws up a little cloud of dust. Then they are off round the corner and out of sight. All that remains is the little cloud of dust. (Dust in the air suspended - marks the place where a story ended?)

I phone Farq and tell him that something has cropped up and that I won't be able to see him later. "You are puzzling me, my dear friend. I expect some sort of explanation tomorrow."

"Tomorrow, Farq," I tell him, "I doubt if I will be in." And then I hang up. I am surely going crazy because Farq is not one to mess about with and he could have me out on my arse if he so chose.

I go for a walk and when out for a walk decide on more booze. I go into my local but get lumbered with one of the bar bores who wants to tell me about the new car he and his wife are buying. It was either the new car or a holiday in the sun he tells me, but they decided it made more sense to have a new car. It wasn't easy he tells me but they knew they couldn't have both. Life's all about choices I tell him.

I escape and call into our local shop and buy a half-bottle of whisky and then I head back into the hills. I perch myself on the stile where earlier I had launched my paper dart, and I sit there for a while drinking. It's still warm out and the view is breathtaking but I really wish there was a phone at hand to check that my wife and boys had arrived safely. My family. (What is she going to tell her parents?) This sort of thing just happens to other people.

But it doesn't.

I can't think straight. My wife has sort of left me and taken my boys with her. I'm messing Farq about and here I am on top of a hill drinking whisky. I'm chasing a rainbow but as well as a pot of gold at the end of it there's something else that I'd rather not think about too deeply. Instead of my boys having me read them a story in bed they've been dragged off sixty-odd miles in a car with their mother having to come out with some crazy story to explain their presence. And Jake asked me did I mind.

I wish I was a chimpanzee.

I sit there for ages until the whisky is finished and it's starting to get dark. It might be dark but at least I can see what I have to do. I have to finish this nonsense. I have to see D tomorrow: what is the alternative? (Listen son, your mum and I are going to be living apart from now on but maybe I'll get to see you the odd weekend. Do you mind?)

Drunk and muddy I decide to call on some neighbours we socialise with. Dick comes to the door in his dressing gown and at first I don't think he's for letting me in.

"Hi, Dick!" I tell him, "The good lady has taken herself and the boys off for a few days so I thought I'd just say hello on the way past." I feel foolish but eventually I'm ushered into his front room. I'm his excuse to bring some beer through from the fridge so he's pleased enough that I called, but his wife is spread out on the couch half-asleep. They have three children - one just a few months old - and they certainly leave their mark. Toys and nappies and all the paraphernalia associated with the rearing of children litter the place. Dick and I trade small talk and he's friendly enough but Carol makes no effort. Carol is whacked by the look of her, and I can smell her feet. She's beside me there on the couch with her bare feet and those feet have had a tough day.

I make myself aware of Dick. He has an old terry-towelling dressing gown on which is a mosaic of breakfast stains and I shudder to think what else. Their house is in a mess and they are a mess and they are married. I have to stop myself, sitting there pissed, from asking them if they are happy. Above the fireplace is a large ostentatious photograph of themselves on their wedding day. A younger Dick and Carol smile down on this scene - this, my friend, *this is your life.*

I realise Dick has been asking me something and is now expecting an answer. I've been miles away. I've been at his wife's feet and his dressing gown and I feel ashamed and patronising for thinking this way.

"Sorry Dick," I tell him, "I was miles away there. I've had a bit to drink tonight."

"You have that," he laughs. "Maybe you should go home and sleep it off. You're in a bit of a mess."

(I'm in a bit of a mess.)

I leave them to it, a muddy carpet my calling card. I'm appalled and confused and I keep hearing my boy asking "Do you mind?" I'm near to tears again as I come in the front door and into my empty house. I check the place for drink and am relieved in a sense that I have none. I go upstairs and collapse into bed, and reflect on the fact that my feet smell just like Carol's.

I'm awake early and am surprised at my lack of headache. I quickly shower and dress and then phone Ann's parents. I am relieved that it is Ann herself who answers. "Everything is going to be fine," I tell her. "I've been a fool. I've had my ego massaged and got carried away." I keep giving her this stuff. "I'm missing you. Hell, I'm missing you and the boys something terrible. So please, come on home." I keep on, but she's not saying too much. She's just going on about it being so early and am I trying to wake the whole household? I tell her again that everything's going to be fine and that I'll call again later, and then she can tell me when she's coming home with my boys.

I try to write D a letter but it's no good. Later on I go to the shop and pick up my newspaper, then I go to the park next to the school and pretend to read. I'm looking out for D. Dear, sweet D - we were not meant to be. It would have been nice to stay as friends, but maybe it's just not possible for men and women to be like that. It's been fun and it's been good for the self-esteem and all that sort of stuff but it's getting to be dangerous, so now it's time to put a stop. In a way I suppose that's what she wants to hear too. So come on D, let's get the goodbyes over with.

I hear the school bell and see all the kids forming into their lines. I saunter over towards the school gate, knowing she'll appear any minute. Then I see her, and she sees me. We wave to each other and she sort of runs up the playground and then she is beside me. The sun is in her face and causing her to squint slightly the way she does and she smiles and whispers a hello, and dear sweet Jesus she is so beautiful . . . she is beautiful and I have that slight dizziness that I get . . . and . . . and . . . she's saying it's so good to see you . . . come up for a coffee . . . everything's going to be fine . . . and our hands sort of brush together and we turn to face each other again and we smile and
God help me,
        God help us.
           God help us all.
Pete Fortune

TALBOT RICE GALLERY

University of Edinburgh,
Old College, South Bridge,
Edinburgh EH8 9YL
Tel: 031 667 1011 x 4308

23 November - 21 December
KEN CURRIE
NEW WORKS

11 January - 29 February 1992
ALAN DAVIE
WORKS ON PAPER

Tues-Sat 10am-5pm, Free.
Subsidised: Scottish Arts Council

SETTLED TERMS

Poems 1965-1989
by David Summers

an edition limited to 200 numbered copies signed by the author, set in Photina and printed on 120 gsm acidfree paper, hardbound in canvas covers with presentation slip-case. £25.00 NET. ISBN 0 951 44910 9

Montpelier Press
15 Montpelier, Edinburgh EH10 4LZ

Setting Forth

A collection of poetry and prose from South Queensferry

Andrew Greig, Jenni Daiches, Sydney Goodsir Smith, Hector MacMillan and others with illustrations from Lindsay Cook

A small book that speaks volumes for a town

£3.00 from
Rivet Publishing
12 East Terrace
South Queensferry
EH30 9HS

Nissim Ezekiel

ADVICE TO MYSELF - 1

That which is truly a burden
may flash its insights
to the patient soul,
and even be
a source of joy.

Narcissus, on the other hand,
never understands
the nature of a burden:
its varied voices,
subtle music,
even when it drags you
close to chaos.

Move freely
among your enactable roles.
Whether light or heavy,
find a way to choose
and be chosen by
those destiny-burdens.

ADVICE TO MYSELF - 2

Once you know the depths,
you cannot live outside them
and know a friend or a book
except as a puzzle clarified.

If you have lost your way,
remember, you are still near
the eternal light and darkness,
not alone. Listen to your silences.

What do you expect? Do not count
your failures and your successes.
Trust the depths. Return to them.
Judge and be judged as part of living.

Let these be your gods, who do not
answer your prayers or tell you how
to save your soul. Assess what they say.
Respect them even if you disagree.

Learn to improvise and celebrate
your own clumsy dances, within
and outside the cave of reality,
shaping, re-ordering your time and space.

BOMBAY TELEPHONES

I did not keep my promise
of giving you, what you called
a tinkle.
First, because I couldn't get
the dial tone;
then because it seemed
your number was engaged
(though I'm sure it wasn't!)
Finally, because I got
the wrong number twice
and felt frustrated -
well, mildly upset.

So, here is my message
(or whatever you call it):
Let us meet
without relying on Bombay Telephones.

Where? When? How?

Well, just give me a tinkle.

Ian Crockatt

ANNIVERSARY
(Wenna's poem)

Some tunes never develop beyond a few bars.
Landlubbers launch expecting to navigate oceans.
It's sad when friends stop loving each other,
when passionate faces contort over lists of possessions
and feelings forced in the hot-house fug of marriage
are weighed in the frosty palms of solicitors.

Mulling you over - humming old themes, sounding new depths -
I find no wicket-gate you've nudged me through has led
to that walled garden where nothing changes,
where I become wholly I and you are completely you -
that graveyard called Eden.
You taught me never to say forever, never

to petrify our lives in glaze, to be dis-satisfied,
restless as waves which come and come again and still crave oceans.
Or is that what I taught you?
We're riding a mare with a sensitive mouth,
she's confident but twitchy, not wholly predictable;
we've a long, maybe a shortening way to go.

And it's twenty years since we started, and I'm
madder now for your body, more in love with unfathomable you,
and we've deserts to cross, and seas, apart, together,
Some nights our dreams go surfing out of control.
Two bodies shape one question-mark under our covers.
Another twenty years, best friend and lover?

THOUGHT-BEASTS

Behind the pretty walls of her head
and its cute shut shutters lies her mind.
Her mind steals out on the limb of itself
searching the darkness with octopus stealth -

and giant squid are said to have dragged
ships down, suckered men under the waves
till terror drowned them, water filled their chests,
and beaks sharp as marlinspikes bloodied their vests.

Her lashes drip distress. Why do the peace-
whales we cherish writhe in nets? May her mind
lie like a billiard-ball, snug
in the pocket of her head. May her adults

search the crannies of her room -
as divers might a sunk ship's hold,
stabbing their torch-beams at eye-glints -
and kill all thought-beasts dead.

COILLIEGHILLIE

If a porpoise
under the gleaming hoop
of its own back
in the rise and the fall

of a seaway
could with its air-vent
do more than breathe, could
vary its husky music

and make melody,
would it be
waltz-time? Pibroch? A shanty?
Coillieghillie,

abandoned, half-saved,
with views to Skye
and the flat hat of Raasay,
on breathless evenings

Illustration to 'The Recruits' by Caroline Hunter

when the sun's low glide
is about to complete
its exquisite chameleon
dyeing of the sea

and oystercatchers' skrilling
and the stonechat's clirk
instinctively cease,
and our breath's stopped too, and

pssssh pssssh pssssh pssssh
porpoises are heard
before they're seen - and we
seem momentarily separate

as two stones - you
summon musings consequential
as these. And then the sky's lid
closes on the sea.

THE RECRUITS

1. Baptism of Thomas the doubter.

To rise streaming love
and run the green road home
- believer, exultant - and burst
in on their dumb ranked lives -
his blowsy son and boorish daughter
and nerve-wracking wife - and shout
"I'll tread the road with Jesus!"
The one clear climax of his life.

2. Fishers of men

I wonder what they told their wives about him,
what were their nagging doubts,
grouped there under the eucalyptus
gutting their glut of fish, steeling
themselves to leave with the miracle-maker;

And whether they could picture him
shouting those innocent words
about being broken, being let down,
up there on his cross in the gruelling heat,
hurt to death by the nails,
begging my God don't let me die
like fishermen clawing their nets in during a storm;
and whether, if they could, they would have gone.

Ian Crockatt

Net of Kins, Web of Ilks:
MacCaig's Phantasmagoria
Jack Rillie

In the last of these poems the train returns the poet over the Border:
>Scotland I rush towards you
>into my future that,
>every minute,
>grows smaller and smaller.

Simply MacCaig's way of waving hello. Hasn't he just said 'I light a cigarette/ and sit smiling in the corner'? So, beyond the index and blank end-papers, in fag-time, another poem dribbles down a page. It will bring, in consonance with his twilit mood, "the salt of absence/ the honey of memory".

This new edition of the *Collected Poems* (Chatto & Windus) reproduces the poems in the 1985 volume, the poems in *Voice-Over* and 15 unpublished poems. In the first edition, MacCaig had thoroughly filleted his published volumes, omitting altogether the earliest Apocalypse volumes. With the unpublished poems he included on that earlier occasion, there are here some 130 unpublished poems covering the period from *Riding Lights* (1955) to the present. We must respect poets' unwishing of parts of their work, and MacCaig cherishes "that power, the truly godlike one,/ of destroying our own creations", but while he may uncreate in his study, what has had its "toilette for eternity" will rise again in the last great day of the *Complete Poems*. For what has been long withheld and now received we may be truly thankful.

It is an impressive *oeuvre*, an achievement earned on its own terms. It has resisted the pressures of public expectations, especially in its failure to fulfil the obligations of an heir to the Scottish Renaissance. He has, it is said, "no big themes" and too many short poems - the connection is causal. He is *degagé* in politics and in religion. The poetry makes none of the usual bids for attention, denying itself the hieratic tone, the high rhetoric, the incantations which homogenise mass feelings. Most of this is true; it is the conclusions and judgments drawn from it which are confused, irrelevant, and aesthetically false. For this is an accomplished poetry, not only in its high technical competence, but in the penetrating gaze it turns on our world, the restless probing intelligence, its generous understanding of the human predicament, its good manners, restraint, and pervasive and underlying gentleness. And its varied musics carry the tonalities of his unmistakable voice. it is a talent many of the greatest poets do not possess. But one *hears* Hardy in this way, and Frost, and Yeats. With its intimacy it brings trust. Yes, an impressive *oeuvre*, a poetry of exquisite attention, its looking informed with love.

As a poet. he carries all the burdens of Modernism - linguistic ague, the collapse of Romantic concord, the 'death of God', the task of making a world whose intelligibility will render it, though without guarantees, a human world. It is with such issues that *Norman MacCaig: Critical Essays* (ed. Joy Hendry and Raymond Ross, EUP), deals. Coinciding with his 80th birthday, the collection, refusing the title of *Festschrift*, is concerned with critical exegesis, though the introduction by Sorley MacLean is a warm, perceptive tribute to the man and his poetry. It valuably supplies a long-needed aid to a proper critical understanding of MacCaig's work in its time, place, and origins.

Of all the allegiances ascribed to MacCaig the label of Apocalyptic groupie seems the most improbable. That he shared some of its mannerism is incontestable, but he had no commitment to its incoherent manifestoes. Thom Nairn, in proposing 'Surrealist', associates him with one element of Apocalypse. It's an attractive term to throw at the "blooming, buzzing confusion" of contradictions and improbables of MacCaig - and Nairn is not backing the suggestion heavily. But seriously - chance, the unconscious, non-rationality? The only likely interest MacCaig may share is the entry in Satie's diary: "My doctor has always told me to smoke. He even explains himself: 'Smoke my friend. Otherwise someone else will do it in your place'." Nairn's main concern, convincingly, is to establish *Surroundings* as the culmination of what MacCaig calls his "long haul towards lucidity". Here the dominating presence of the "real MacCaig" - his interest in "the nature of the mind/ and the process of observing" - finds expression in "the sparse, incisive cohesion that has come to characterise MacCaig's work". He sees the emerging influence of Stevens, and a deepening concern with language and its flakiness:

> So far from being silenced
> he wrote more poems than ever
> and all of them different -
> just as a stoned crow
> invents ways of flying
> it had never thought of before.

It is a simile MacCaig will take with him wherever he flies.

Given MacCaig's rejection of his Apocalyptic beginnings, it would have been unsurprising if he had found a natural home among the Movement poets. A poetry which, in Conquest's words, is to display 'empirical' attitudes. "reverence for the real person or event", "a rational structure and a comprehensible language", would not be alien even to the MacCaig of the Eighties. But dared by Donald Davie to be "anything but numb" is not quite his temper, nor that febrile mix of neutrality and revolt which set so much of the tone of that period in English culture. Angus Calder's careful discriminations return what seem like Movement features in MacCaig to personal and native influences. He discerns "A distinctive 'voice' . . . that of a representative unaccommodated human being . . . neither academic (sic) nor class-conscious", neither 'preaching' like Auden, nor 'domineering' like Hughes. But Calder is perhaps over-anxious to trace MacCaig's roots to Scottish, or, save the Metaphysicals, to un-English soil - in Gaelic, John Anderson and Grieve, Montgomerie, the Classics. But surely no-one content to write poetry in English in MacCaig's life-time could have been deaf to the tones of Auden (cf 'Dream World' and 'Lay your sleeping head, my love . . .') or his greater predecessors, or to the 'New Poets' whose company he kept in Alvarez's Penguin anthology. And he listened to Wallace Stevens and listened good.

It is difficult to spot specific Scottish influences on MacCaig. Watching

Scots critics picking over a writer's DNA to find traces of Calvin, Dunbar, Hume or Scott isn't a pretty sight, as if literary value depended on purity of strain. How disturbing to reflect that, in digesting Stevens, MacCaig may have among his chromosomes, Bergson, Whitehead, Santayana - but a few of the alien intruders. John MacInnes's 'MacCaig and Gaeldom' is not guilty of these misapprehensions. He makes no attempt to avoid MacCaig's disavowals of making use of Gaelic metres: "Gaelic is a language I do not speak". There is enough topographical reference, a developed taste for pibroch, chanter and fiddle, to establish his strong affections for the North and concern for its people and their history. Seeing MacCaig as 'The History Man' Raymond Ross develops these interests, demonstrating a wide-ranging awareness of history as it "impinges on the individual", sharply engaged in the context of Gaeldom, sceptical of the "big words" of politics. There is no aesthetically active 'historical sense' as in Eliot, no troping of history as in Muir, nor a DIY system in the manner of Yeats. Nor is the absence of such features a defect, but before taking too seriously the 'History Man' label it is better to understand that the modes of MacCaig's interests in history are in fact pretty general.

Two important influences Joy Hendry deals with in 'The Classsical and Metaphysical Humours of Norman'. ('Humours' is so right!) The poetry is well-sown with classical references, but she warily recognised that its assimiliation will manifest itself in "nuance and subtlety". Still, her text from the Greek Anthology is no bad place to start; "Thunder is not my job, that's for Zeus". There could be more of MacCaig there than in any formal echoes the critical Asdic might pick up. She attests his warm admiration for Plato, the Socrates of the *Phaedo* especially, although she discerns no specific philosophical influence within the poetry itself. (It is surprising that there is no trace of the linguistic debate in the *Cratylus*.) Since Platonism takes her to "metaphysics" - before the term's misuse as a label for 17th century poets - she sensibly dismisses the idea of MacCaig as a "metaphysician". The "strong lines" of these poets are a quite different matter and she eliminates from MacCaig's debt that poetry's drama as well as its exhaustive exploitation of the conceit. "Simply to state his position is his concern"; no persuasion, and no seduction. However, she finds justification for the label in his "preoccupation with the self and its relation with the not-self" - in "the Hegelian fashion of the Real..." Yet *is* all this, in act, so to speak, in its *poetic* behaviour, "metaphysics" or epistemology, or *sprachphilosophie* - or maybe, in the true sense of its 17th century usage, *ludic* "metaphysics"?

While ultimate questions may be metaphysical or phenomenological, the reductionism of most contemporary thinking has brought everything down to questions about language. And it is to the medium itself that MacCaig addresses his existential questions. Christopher Whyte deals the central issue of figured language in 'This Trash of Metaphor'. He sees MacCaig as having a love/hate attitude to metaphor which, in its doubleness of tenor and vehicle, prevents things being just what they are. "He longs for a world of mere identity", yet declares "I by metaphor/ share the world's sharing..." But again ('No Choice') "(I am growing, as I get older,/ to hate metaphors - their exactness/ and their inadequacy.)" A preference for nouns over adjectives, or metaphors, Whyte interprets as a desire to classify, separate, while adjectives blur distinctions. And metaphor, with its "is" and "seems", exacerbates the confusion, yet the poet - or the primordial language itself - is addicted to it. But if nouns are, as Whyte puts it, "guiltless", names should be even more secure. But names too are queer, and in poems like '1,800 feet up' the creatures themselves are not in possession of their names. Beyond language then? "The language of touch, the speechless/ vocabulary of hands". Whyte notes that this obviously "metaphorises the beyond-language as another kind of language". Yawing thus between detachment and belonging, as Whyte sees it, MacCaig finds "salvation" "momentarily" in human reciprocity. It is a meticulous piece of criticism with extensive technical examination of the poet's use of metaphor. There are, nevertheless, matters of emphasis, procedure, and conclusions which give a mistaken view of the poetry and the poet.

Firstly, he may be taking too solemnly MacCaig's somersaulting antics on metaphor, naming, language, detachment. That the poem expresses conviction does not mean that it is a survival issue for the poet. It may be a strategy which allows us to see and him to use both sides of a coin. That many of these examples are trivial pursuits - like "water trickling down a wall or/ a wall being trickled down by water" suggests that he is not hunting epistemological game nor in deep linguistic or perceptual distress. What is on display here are the processes of poetry - in the Coleridgean terms of the mind "*Active* in perception", imagination dissolving, diffusing, dissipating, "in order to recreate", and all "awakening the mind from the lethargy of custom".

My second point is connected with the way MacCaig is perceived as altogether too cool, aloof, intellectually cold. (I cannot think that any diligent reading of the *Collected Poems* could sustain that impression.) Whyte, however, quite legitimately, takes his discussion of metaphor beyond the epistemological issue into the wider area of relationships in MacCaig, the psychological tensions which surface in the idiolect. "The impossibility of any truly detached perspective is felt as a tragedy in much of MacCaig's work." The "chill sternness" found in MacCaig he traces from his usages - the preference for the "guiltless" noun as against the blurring togetherness of metaphor for example - where he finds a deep desire for "separateness". The metaphors are rarely "sensuous", and vision, dominant in MacCaig, is "least sensual". He is said to prefer, as subjects, animals to people as eliciting no, or weak, emotional response. "Nor does he seek similitudes for what it feels like to feel things (what it is to have you hold me in your arms . . .)."

It is a formidable charge, and by no means flimsily constructed. The bleak conclusion is not however the only one which fits the facts. It rests to a considerable extent, I believe, on an extensive misreading of the tone of the poems. The comment on 'Visiting Hour' is not untypical: "The avoidance of emotion becomes conscious: 'I will not feel, I will not/ feel, until/ I have to'." I find these lines dramatically convincing, for not only is the desperation of the denial an assertion of feeling, but the rest of the poem dramatises poignantly the pressure of feeling which has to be controlled. Nor is it *literally* the case in 'Linguist' that his "declarations of love have fallen to the level of animal noises". The serious point of the serio-comic performance as he goes "dingdonging and mooing my way/ through all the lexicons and languages/ of imprecision" is in the "despairing anthology of *praises*, a concentration of all the *opposites of reticence.*" (Jug Jug is not only for *dirty ears.*) Surely the poem is about the inadequacy of our love-*talk*, not of our love. But the poetry is packed with denials which are affirmations, withdrawals which are advances, filling the abstract with the extravagant copiousness of creation and "the gaiety of language". What, significantly, 'Go-between' is asserting is that "the finality of form", however "classical", conceals or has to include "the lunacy of form" - "owl's hoot, exploding salmon . . ."

Roderick Watson's text, "Noticing you can do nothing about/ It's the balancing that shakes the mind" is a corrective to Whyte's misreadings. Concentrating on the later poems Watson points to the "note of personal, almost confessional intimacy", while deferring to Iain Crichton Smith's denial that it is only the death of friends which has made MacCaig more aware of mortality. "What has happened", Smith says, "is that in the later poems the disguises have been stripped away to a greater degree than before." Indeed in his "noticing" and "balancing" Watson finds the "weight of joy" and the "weight of sadness" of these last poems as early as the New Apocalypse. But age brings "Wakings" more frequently "Ugly", and Karamazov's brutal questions haunt "the role of an Alternative Creator . . . who tries to justify (make sense of) the world in his work." The long-serving linguistic sceptic meets "words/ with no meaning, words like *consolation,/* words like *goodbye.*" Watson speaks of 'On the Beach' as "somewhere between absurd comedy and linguistic desperation". But the latter is a conventional element of the former, in Ionesco say, or in Beckett. He can't go on. He goes on.

It is what has to be done in a world of flux: demanding from Stevens, as from MacCaig, "the endlessly elaborating poem", a poetry in, and of, process. So he confronts "the gaudy tangle" (Pater) of changeful reality and finds:

> Being expressing itself - as it does in its continuous
> Its never-ending creation of leaves,
> birds, waves, stone boxes - and beliefs
> true and false.

He is not in Stevens's sense a "fictionalist" but when Stevens says "the final belief is to believe in a fiction which you know to be a fiction, there being nothing else" he could well be describing MacCaig's 'strategies'. And living in a world in process he shares the compulsion felt by writers from Wordsworth on to find forms, heuristic devices, which will acknowledge flux while preserving the comforting solidity of the self and its familiar world. The gerund, combining the dynamic function of the verb with the stasis of the noun becomes a fairly common usage. Hopkins's 'Inscape' or 'Doing-Be' has a gerundial force. There are in MacCaig 'windings', 'journeyings', 'waterlispings' and kindred forms - 'steeplejacking', 'Rollsroycing'. But his most characteristic response arises from the need for "a never-ending/ exclamation. a single word, like the first one,/ of continuous creation, of difficult universes".

His geometries. almost Platonic infrastructures of Being from the *Timaeus* - angles, lines, triangles, circles, diagrams, patterns - will, as design. draw together the shifting appearances and present, with startling confidence and permanence, a Blue Jar, say. "It holds out a truth/ on a fiction." The music of the harpsichords in 'Down-to-earth heaven' "make it possible/ to believe in the original Word that changed/ being to becoming." The poems go back on several occasions to Adam, the Creator's surrogate, the giver of names in Eden with no "other", no "shameless demander of similes, the destroyer of Eden." But the sons of Adam have no longer the authority of naming. The Logos is no more, and everything is "undecidable". This is MacCaig's territory, and everything is also possible. Epistemology? Phenomenology? Hegel? Vienna Circle? Something more like a *paysage moralisé* perhaps.

That his poems are the strikes and spoil from working the great fault in perception is obvious. What is less certain is whether hermeneutics is on the right track in tracing its origins and purposes to systematic philosophy, or in giving it a philosophical coherence. And he likes to show philosophers a good deal of disrespect. MacCaig instinctively twigged, long before young novelists discovered the "Funhouse", that Cassirer's "Animal Symbolicum" was simply a pretentious facade for "Homo Ludens", or perhaps that the latter is an inevitable kenosis of the former. And Nietzsche had already asserted that "the deepest pathos is still aesthetic play". The ludic impulse is in grain in MacCaig - one has only to hear the voice ironising the poems. Sometimes it is an irresponsible mischief. At times he is the Cretan Liar, or pretends to be, or, more confusingly, wonders whether he is. It is also one of the most important convictions he shares with Stevens that "Life's nonsense pierces us with strange relation". For "nonsense" in both poets is a sophisticated image of the necessary "play" of the imagination in exercising its freedom.

Those features we call his "epistemology", or "phenomoenology" are more properly to be taken as what Yeats called the poet's "phantasmagoria". "A poet . . ." he says, "never speaks directly as to someone at the breakfast table, there is always a phantasmagoria. Dante and Milton had mythologies . . ." and Yeats had his "History". In MacCaig's case we might say it was the Epistemological Spirits who came to give him, like Yeats, "metaphors for poetry". It provides MacCaig with a choreography in which a continuous dialogue of the mind with itself and with every otherness links poem to poem and is never closed. Conclusion will be a halting, an aporia, a defeat, a despair - "I will be left with only/ The loneliness of falling" and the next poem will begin "the mountains fold and move/ I'm not quite lost". Syllogism, sorites, paradox, chiasmus, postulate, - these are the counterpart as figures of thought with, for example, his geometries. They trace the design or spangle the pattern, elements in the great bamboozlement of man, in any position.

And the dialectic is a drama, comic, wry, "Absurd Comedy". It allows him to rejoice in the "decor of being", phenomena and noumena commuting freely. Or he may rend metaphor and demand the world in its selfhood - glacier, water, bread, wood . . . reference unjeopardised. Beyond that, in the ultimate exhausted silence, as with Lowell he "talks extinction to death", there is "the language of touch, the speechless/vocabulary of hands" (where Virgil should leave him and the poet go on alone - but doesn't). We do not ask what he *really* believes. Hegel, Husserl, Moore, Freud jostle with frogs, caterpillars, gulls, roses, Mrs Grant, the live and the loving, the dying and the dead, all within that high glaze, that blessed aesthetic distance where alone everything can BE, the artifice that is our only version of eternity.

Jack Rillie

Cartoon of Norman MacCaig and Eddie Linden by Gerald Mangan

Norman MacCaig

So many worlds

I stand for a few minutes
at the mouth of Hell's Glen.
Not because I think there are devils in it
and generations of the dead
being tortured for the sins they can't forget.

Behind me the loch I know so well
smiles in the sun and laughs along its shores.
It is part of my Paradise -
with not a saint in it
no harps twangling
their endless tunes.

Always between two worlds,
Hell's Glen and Paradise
and that's not counting those inside me
where the moon brushes its way
through groves of birch trees
and ice floes ignore those silent dancers
in the midnight sky
and cities that have died
send their ghosts into the streets of Edinburgh
and the word she spoke changed my darkness
to a summer morning, friendly as a fireside.

Poems for her

Take from me these toys I've made
with shells from the depth of the sea.

Aphrodite was born there
from the sea that washed the shores
that Homer dreamt about.

My little baubles would never grace
the neck, the arms of Aphrodite.
Nor will they yours.

But maybe you'll think
of the calm depths
from which I wrested them,

Maybe you'll recognise truths
I could never speak
and look at me
with new knowledge; with a little wonder?

Some people are never satisfied

I sawed down the tree
and left an apple up there
where it had always been.

People came in droves
and gaped at it.
Extraordinary, they said.

I chopped up the tree
for firewood
And burned it.

And people still came
and stared at the apple
and said, Amazing. Fantastic.

Except for one small boy
who only called out
Can you put the tree back,
mister?

Languages

A dragonfly speaks to me
in its own language
whose verbs and nouns
are shimmers of four wings
and dazzles of blue.

The little stream it flies beside
talks in lyrics made
of the curves and curlicues of water.

Even the grasses,
those imperturbable philosophers,
explain in solemn paragraphs
how to change
from one green to another.

And my language? - Sounds in the air
and scribbles on paper:
and in good days each make
a brassbound strongbox
of things I remember.

A sort of thanks

My memory's getting slipshod.

Yet it still suddenly reveals
the mile-long bank of primroses
by Loch Sal, last Spring. Or it produces
from nowhere the acrobatic pair of ravens
I saw near Drumbeg so many years ago.

Like a lost ship that reaches harbour in a fog
memory unloads cargoes from hundreds of ports -
bales of words, bundles of people,
a treasure chest of music - lamps
better than Aladdin's.
Memory, I've not destroyed you yet
and never will -
for whoever heard of a bird
wrecking its own nest?
Whoever heard of a bird
plucking out its own flight feathers?

In the house called The Glen

Where now are the gloomy thoughts? . . .

Outside the new lambs
are nuzzling their mothers
and a freezing wind is saying
Stay indoors.

I will.
And peace, that old-fashioned thing,
settles on the sofa
and looks at me with forgotten eyes.

I love her gray hair
and her hands clasped in her lap
as though holding a precious thing -
and talking with a quiet voice
that drowns the noisy world
with its gloomy thoughts
and hectoring demands.

It's night now.
I've no fear of falling asleep.
I've no fear of waking in the morning.
For peace will say, Today
is like yesterday
and I'll be here for the long length of it.

April 1991

Yesterday, for the first time this year,
I was in the Borders
with its green hills and fields.

Memory became alert -
those rivers I've fished, little towns
that always look newly Spring cleaned
and a friendly house in Ancrum
with daffodils everywhere.

But what I specially remembered
are the tiny lambs who had lived
for not many hours
calling 'Mammy'
if they were ten feet from their mothers
and tottering towards them on knees like knots
that need tightening.

And all to become sheep
with nothing to do but eat
and nothing to eat but grass
and to end up
in a scatter of butchers' shops.

Trapped

Man, frantic with admiration
for the gray mess inside his skull,
invented the wheel, which turned into
a bicycle and a fighter plane and on and on . . .

He invented hygiene, which turned into
interesting new diseases.

He invented an afterlife and can't wait
to go into it

Look - a new thought has appeared
in the brain of Professor Cedilla.
He doesn't know it, but it's shaped
like a boomerang and it knows
where it's going.

Normam MacCaig

Literary Life in Edinburgh #6: The Small Hours chez McCaig

"Start an argument Gerry, for God's sake."

Norman MacCaig, Brian McCabe, Tom Pow, Alan Taylor, Gerald Mangan

Changing Places
Mary E Edward

The pub door had been painted; a hard lacquered black. He reached out to push the brass door plate and he could see the moving reflection of his hand. His fingers made little islands of damp on the smooth metal.

Inside, the pub was dark. Apart from shafts of coloured light which scythed across each other from some hidden source far above. Smoke, trapped inside the columns of light, swirled with an urgency which seemed to keep time with the loud music. He could feel the sound beating through the soles of his shoes. In the strange glow he could make out white face shapes, and mouths - opening and closing - but no words. Malcolm began to feel dizzy. He wanted to leave but his legs were shaking and he knew that he would fall if he tried to turn back to the door and the daylight.

When his eyes adjusted to the gloom he edged sideways until he reached a seat. He leaned on it to sit down and the seat was covered with a material which was warm to the touch. The raised fibres responded comfortably to his digging fingernails. He placed his other hand on the table and the surface was cold: the bumpy ceramic glittered with points of light and the table top seemed watery and insubstantial. He drew his hand away and shuffled along the bench until his body came into contact with the wall. Whirls of plaster pressed into his shoulder. Locked into the corner Malcolm tried to think about how he came to be in the wrong place.

He thought about the street outside. He remembered passing the post office and the fruit shop. Boxes leaning against the green wall and white cards with blue writing. Golden Delicious - 6 for 40p. The paler green of the apples and one or two wrapped in tissue paper as if they were special. And he remembered the sign for bananas which had too many 'n's. But when he'd looked inside the shop it had been a dark man in a turban instead of Cissie Lang. Still, the shop was the same and the cobbler's was still next door to it. Even if there were handbags and dogs' leads in the window where there used to be a big iron last in a dusty space. And packets of segs. Inside, piles of shoes upside down on a shelf, and an inky smell. Then the dairy was next door to the cobbler's. Malcolm's stomach thudded and his face began to burn. He couldn't remember seeing the dairy.

The post office - the fruit shop - the cobbler's - the dairy...then Lafferty's pub. The door facing diagonally on to the street corner and high brown walls. On summer nights voices and the smell of beer puffing out and the door held open by a big round stone with a handle on it. Once he'd asked his father what it was and he said it was a curling stone. For a long time Malcolm had wondered what it was supposed to curl.

He sat in the dark corner and the music thumped into his skull. He closed his eyes and tried to picture the dairy. His head began to ache and he covered his face with his hands and thought hard about how he came to be in the wrong place.

There was movement near him and a clean, tangy scent leaked between his closed fingers. He took his hands away. Two people were standing at the other side of the table. A young chap and a girl. they were looking at him and the boy waved a pointing finger over the table. Malcolm shook his head. The boy spoke to the girl and she sat down, then he walked over to the bar. When he stood in the funny light it made a halo round his hair and his white jacket was purple and luminous. It reminded Malcolm of stained glass. He shifted his eyes to the girl and she smiled - a little smile. He thought the girl and boy were very young to be in a pub.

Red-faced men always spilled out of Lafferty's Public House at half-past-nine on Saturday nights. Then they would stand on the pavement in swaying groups, talking and arguing. Sometimes there would be shouting and holding each other back - and the dark police van. Once, he'd heard a woman crying and the raw noise had made his insides tremble.

On Sundays he'd been awed by the deserted silence around the closed pub when they passed in the morning on the way to church. Malcolm walking between his father and his mother. His blazer, his grey trousers and his best top hose. And a clean vest, taken off the wire strung along the mantelpiece, smelling of the fish they always had for their tea on Saturdays. His mother's grip on his hand tightening when they came to Lafferty's.

The boy came back to the table and gave the girl a tall glass. The drink was yellow, like custard, and it had a paper umbrella floating in it by the stick. The boy had a mug of beer. The girl picked the umbrella out of the glass and flicked it - open and shut - open and shut - at the boy. He ducked and laughed as a few tiny drops of the yellow liquid hit his face. He put his arm around the girl and grabbed the umbrella from her, then he pushed it into her hair. She let it stay for a moment, then she pulled it out and laid it closed on the table. It looked like a dead butterfly. The girl smiled openly at Malcolm as she shook her long hair and her soft young face made him think of Nurse Carson at the hospital. The long hair was different though.

None of the nurses had long hair, but the young woman who had come to talk to Malcolm about leaving had long frizzy hair and big round specs. Going back into the community, she said, was good for people like Malcolm. Her name was Ginny and she had come to see how he was getting on in the flat. The flat. When his mother was alive it had been a room and kitchen.

The girl laid her hand on the boy's shoulder and put her mouth close to his ear. He listened, lifted his beer mug and pointed at it, nodding to Malcolm and saying something. Malcolm thought he was offering to buy him a drink. He hesitated, then nodded back and the boy got up from the table.

Malcolm gripped the handle of the mug and wrapped his other hand around the curving glass. His fingers fitted into the cold dimples. The beer got warmer as he drank. It took him a long time. They never had beer at the hospital. But when they were taken out to the town they'd been allowed to have a drink after they'd practised the shops. Preparing To Live In The Community. One hundred pennies in a pound. Sugar, tea and bacon . . .

His mother always made the bacon and eggs when they came back from the church at dinnertime. Malcolm looked forward to it . . . and the tattie scones. Then there was the quietness until they had their tea and went to the evening service. He remembered how still it was. His father with his jacket on, reading the hard, dark books he got from the library on Fridays. His mother, head bent over silent embroidery. And Malcolm's bible stories rustling like little waves on a shore as he turned the pages, one by one. His father looking up at him when there was the sound of play from the backcourt far below.

After his father was killed the house was never as quiet again. On any day. Not just on the day it happened and the foreman came to tell his mother how the hawser had snapped away from the capstan on the ship. Nor at the funeral when his father's workmates tramped into the house, caps twisting in their hands. No. Afterwards his mother would put on the wireless, quietly, on Sunday afternoons. Or sometimes she'd take him to the park, and for a Macallum in Gallone's. The raspberry on the white ice cream ran like blood - Malky Reid . . . yer faither loast his heid . . . Malky Reid . . . yer faither . . .

His beer mug was empty and he wanted to go to the toilet. He shuffled in the seat but he couldn't see the right door. There were a lot of people standing now, blocking his view. He could see a pale door with a wee cut-out doll which was supposed to be a woman. The figures on the hospital doors were black, but this one was shiny brass like the plate outside. A girl pushed the door open and the doll shimmered - from gold to red to blue to gold.

Malcolm pressed the palms of both hands hard down on the watery table top and leaned on it to stand up. He tried not to look into the shifting light and the crush of bodies. The throbbing music seemed to rise with him and he fell back into the seat. He was sweating. He wanted to take off his coat. His fingers, small and childish looking, curled over his left cuff while he tried to pull the other arm out of its sleeve until it jammed at the elbow. He stopped, trapped, and he could feel the sweat cold on his brow.

The girl nudged her boyfriend and he got up and came round the table. Smiling, he pulled the sleeve until Malcolm's arm was free. His cardigan slipped off his shoulder along with the coat and the boy put it back, then he helped him to stand. He pointed over the heads of the people and, taking hold of Malcolm's arm, led him towards the crowds and the blades of light. The boy was tall and pushed a path into the darkness of the packed bodies.

The toilet door swung shut. The noise was cut to a muffled beating. Malcolm's ears buzzed in the quietness. The fluorescent light bounced off the white tiles and hurt his eyes. There was a row of urinals and a smell of disinfectant mixed with urine. Like the hospital. In the bare light the boy was big and powerful-looking and his jacket was very white as he stretched out his arms and put his hands on Malcolm's shoulders.

There was a polished metal bottle on a swing attachment above the wash hand basin. When he pushed the bottom it turned upside down and globules of greenish soap dropped out. Malcolm was too slow the first time and the soap missed his hands and slithered down the side of the sink until it disappeared into the blackness below. In the gleaming metal of the moving bottle Malcolm's elongated face swung towards him and away . . . towards him and away . . .

He looked in the mirror and the boy was still behind him, smiling, waiting.

Mary E Edward

ScAN

THE LIVING TRADITION

A review of folk, traditional and heritage arts in Scotland

Reviews of books, records, videos, concerts, theatre, exhibitions; articles on Scottish Folk Arts activity from Freddie Anderson, Margaret Bennett, David Clement, Sheila Douglas, Dave Hardy, Hamish Henderson, Adam McNaughtan, Aonghas MacNeacail...

Scottish Folk Arts Group
49 Blackfriars Street
Edinburgh, EH1 1NB
Tel: 031 557 3090. Fax: 031 557 5115
Bi-monthly, £1.50, inc p&p

Gairfish

Cohesive collections of high quality essays and poetry.

SCOTLAND: MAPS AND LEGENDS. MacDiarmid and Morgan; Neil Gunn as nationalist provocateur; Scottish cowardice; English racism; General Roy.
Jan 1990 ISBN 0951541900 £3.50

DISCOVERY. The gelding of Robert Burns; stepping back to John Buchan; the strange case of G. Gregory Smith; Frank O'Hara; Schopenhaeur and Darwin.
Nov 1990 ISBN 095151919 £3.50

THE ANARCHY OF LIGHT. Essays in celebration of Neil M. Gunn's centenary.
March 1991 ISBN 0951541927 £3.50

Poems in English, Scots and Gaelic.

Edited by W.N. Herbert and Richard Price
45 Hazelwood Road, Bridge-of-Weir, Strathclyde, PA11 3DX

"Full of absorbing contributions" Neal Ascherson

"Books in Scotland **meets a great need and meets it well."**

BOOKS IN SCOTLAND

A comprehensive and stimulating quarterly review of new books by Scottish writers, books about Scotland and books in general.

Books in Scotland rides no hobby-horses, political or literary. It is an impartial guide appealing to the general reader, to librarians, teachers, students, writers and everyone who uses books for information, study or pleasure.

The surest way of regularly receiving *Books in Scotland* is to become a subscriber.

The Annual Subscription is only £8.95 or £9.95 abroad. Please use this order form.

Please send the next four issues of **Books in Scotland** to:

Mr, Mrs, Miss ....

....

....

....

I enclose cheque/MO for

£   made out to:

The
RAMSAY HEAD PRESS
**15 Gloucester Place,
Edinburgh EH3 6EE, Scotland**

Duncan Glen

ANOTHER DAWN

A time to be peripatetic beneath the Meadows' trees.

It is yesterday's tomorrow today, mebbe!
On Jawbone Walk a man fat with layers of clothes
for sleeping rough says, "scuse me".
I pey nae heed.

The windows of the Royal Infirmary to be passed,
staring een raising my own desert places.

There the evening star ahint the auld trees
green with memories, the bairn to its mither
aye to be diminished by the bright dawn. It is
auburn-haired lass on her wedding day. My mother.

A memory cried to another dawn to set with me.

In the clear northern licht see her deep blue eyes
as violets coloured by the azure sky. But
where these flowers broke through the frozen ground
now passes night and day a coffin.

And yet too a young bride.
And the leaves of the violets seen hairt-shaped.

RYCHRAGGAN

We are going through Glen Urquhart
out of our eyes in our enlightened minds
by Milton and Polmaily. That IS
Saint Maile's Pool! THEN

a sign pointing to the right up a hill
RHYCHRAGGAN
B & B
3/4 OF A MILE.

It is a steep twisting forest of a road,
going on for ever in a highland day
in that three-quarter of a mile.
But we arrive at Rychraggan, Slope of the Rock.

Ducks walk across as we arrive at the cottage's
gable end. We pass through a wrought-iron gate
and go by gravelled path to the front door.
We knock and wait.

A scene glorious as any twelfth day
down the glen
to a glimpse of a rectangle of Loch Ness
with the sun beating out of a cover of blue sky above.

The hills a hazed backcloth for eyes on their unculled
stocks. At our feet a garden enclosed by stone dyke,
richly-coloured with a bed of annual flowers,
orange, red, purple, white and green.

And over the wall, to the right, on the moorland,
a rowan tree heavy with berries looks older than its years.
A group of young crows on the wall rise into the sky. They
swoosh and swirl, turning on their many selves,

the sky alive with their triangulated, silhouetted
wings. A shot cracks the silence out on the hill. The crows
float in their space. Down the glen the loch
has moved in its own waves.

At the door Mrs Macdonald stands to welcome us.

LORDS OF CREATION

Some did it in the beginning
- of the Renaissance -
creating heaven and earth in paint and stone
and language.

And Dante keeked owre ither Florentine waw.
See above the cypresses
                towers and cupola
in the sky that red streak seen in many a painting.

A skywalker before the reality seen seeming like
a creation of art. The renaissance painters taking
the tinted dust of the ground and breathing into oil paint
the breath of life, and each became a *living* god.

And these Lords of Creation said, in Attic order,
"Let us make God in our own image."

The image in head and heart, love and beauty;
together you hold and kindle
beyond time or place
with other fire, with other wings you move.

Not otherwise was Daedalus wakened
not otherwise was Venus born
not otherwise the sun that reveals heich and laich
light and shadow

Illustration to 'The Lords of Creation' by George Elston

naked stone and yirdly flesh.

On the sixth day the Lords of Creations
looked upon their work
and saw that it *was* good but not
good enough.

Daedalus unbound, as Michelangelo carves stone . . .
Venus rises from the sea, as Titian paints colorito . . .
And Beatrice smiles, as Dante scrieves beyond language . . .

The Lords of Creation spoke amongst themselves.
"Perhaps he divided the light too much from the darkness?"
"Perhaps he saw the light in the wrong light?"
"Perhaps he mixed the wrong dust?" "That could not be!"

."Perhaps we need a new image?"

And God drew another breath
but did not waste it.

Duncan Glen

Tachair and the Thumping Majority
(Continued from Chapman 65)

Innis Macbeath

As the autumn schedules, 1990, came in, it was apparent that the television producers were anxious to drop *Tales of Tachair* for a new soap with better viewer-appeal. Impending war, economic collapse and the eclipse of the communist menace fail to improve the ratings, and to recapture its grip on the floundering nation, the Vile Morass pencils in a new face. Tachair says: "I love the work; and I work vereh hard," but this misfires among the unemployed and enhances her reputation as pitiless wretch.

We left the Welsh wizards, Heseltine (*Easach-tighinn* = "Cascades coming") and Howe (Yowe, the somnolescent sheep) quivering on the edge of revolt. With perfect anticlimax, it is Yowe who strikes first. Breaking away from the flock, he sheepishly complains that Tachair has broken his bat, knowing that nothing is more treacherous in the English demonology. Easach-tighinn sees that the time has come to put the cascades under Tachair. In the ensuing contest she secures 204 votes against his 152 and is persuaded to accept defeat. Two of her satraps come out of the shadows and one of them, John Major, miraculously vanquishes Easach-tighinn with 185 votes. From this Thumping Majority the series takes its name.

Some critics are mystified by this touch of the barely credible, but older ones reminisce about democracy at Cambridge University in the 1930s. The students of Oxford had voted, "This house refuses to fight for King and country". A young Willie Whitelaw and militant friends guarded the door at Cambridge to keep out potential voters for a similar resolution. In old age Whitelaw thought this had as much to do with the motion's failure as the eloquence of W S Churchill speaking against it. From this derives Whitelaw's rule of thumb: "Never mind the majority, feel the thump," and just before the decisive thump in 1990 is a scene where Whitelaw is shown ringing a handbell with a sort of demented joy. Tachair makes the memorable observation, "Every Prime Minister needs a Willie.", though she does not seem to know for whom the bell tolls.

This density of satire defies the analysis even of those with knowledge of Haddington, the threefold interment of St Baldred, doing the Lambeth Walk, and *Dr Jekyll and Mr Hyde*. Let us begin with the historical John Major (1469-1550). He is born at Gleghornie in East Lothian and from school in Haddington goes to study at the universities of Cambridge and Paris, returning to Scotland laden with the plaudits of the academic world - "holden," according to John Knox, "as an oracle on matters of religion", "the veritable chief of the scholastic philosophy," and to someone else, one "whose learning will commend him not only to posterity but to all eternity", one who "flies on his own wings higher than the clouds would carry him, till he passes above all spirits in sublimity". Even at one of Tachair's festivals of adulation ("party conferences"), the tributes come no more warmly.

More cautious voices, Melanchthon, for instance, considers Major's writings "a wagonload of trifles - what pages he fills with dispute whether horsemanship requires a horse, whether the sea was salt when God made it, &c". Rabelais, a student when Major is the principal lecturer at the Sorbonne, dreams up for his "Library of St Victor" a book called *Major on the Art of Making Puddings*, and this obscure echo of the Tachair twin sets off a total change of plotting. The Gaeltacht is forgotten; we are instead in a world of mirrors and dissolving boundaries of space and time.

In 1521 is published *A History of Greater Britain, as well England as Scotland*, by John Major (by name a Scot but by profession a theologian), written in Latin and printed in Paris. To anyone who feels this an inclination towards independence in Europe, it should be explained that the historical John Major wishes to see Scotland and England united, if only to stop their fighting each other, and believes that England would never impose unacceptable taxes on Scotland. Like Aillse and others, he is a great one for bells, observing: "There is in England a great plenty of bells of the finest quality; because in the material for making bells England abounds." He also distinguishes two kinds of Scots, the Wild Scots and the Civilised Scots respectively (impudently putting Gleghornie among the latter).

The TV John Major is an anti-hero, a negative of his historical namesake with enough in common to keep on the same photographic plate. He is a sharp break with the discarded Tachair in general bearing and address. and actually born in the Vile Morass, a notion to bring a quiver to the stiffest upper lip.

Once and Future Major

To understand how all the adulation and authority is summarily transferred to an inarticulate bank clerk with an imperfect command of English, we must remember that the historical John Major, great though he is, is a child of his time. He accepts Aristotle's absurd assertion that the people of the north may be spirited but they lack intelligence and skill.

Among the supernatural oddments recorded in the *History* is the multiplication of St Baldred in the sixth century. "It is related of him that his body was laid entire in three churches not far distant one from the other: Aldhame namely, Tyninghame and Preston, of which the first two named are villages distant from Gleghornie about one thousand paces; the third, one league. In these three places St Baldred taught the people by word and example, and on his death all three fell to arms in strife for the possession of his body. The same body was found numerically in different parts of the house, and thus each of these villages rejoices to this day in the possession of St Baldred's body. I know that there are not wanting theologians who deny that such a thing as this is possible to God, namely, that the same body can be placed *circumscriptive* in different places; but their proof of this I cannot allow, as I have shown at more length elsewhere." (Edinburgh, 1892.)

If a body can be in several places at once, he can also be in several times (or even eras) at once. *So John Major keeps cropping up.* There is John Major of Eck, in Swabia, a doughty opponent of Martin Luther; a Belgian Jesuit, flourishing two generations later; and there is John Major the bookseller who produces pretty editions of *The Compleat Angler* but mishandles his business and has to live on charity in the Charterhouse about 150 years ago. The present tense is used to emphasise the unity of John Major transcending space and time as a multi-faceted creature, expressed in different contingencies; perhaps the best analogy is that the Sage of Gleghornie is, so to speak, an academic Dr Jekyll to the TV soap's Mr Hyde. Given the perverse appetites of the viewing public, this distasteful invention proves popular, rather as the bigot Alf Garnett or the villainous J R Ewing found a place in the warped affections of square-eyed soapwatchers.

We must tie up the loose ends left by writing out Tachair. There is a nauseating episode in which Tachair as a minor partner with Recana's successor, Badwine Bush, bushwhack an enemy in the manner of ancient Romans in Gaul, ending the affair in two or three days. The capital community poll charge tax controversy continues to attract universal ribaldry from Kinnock (cnoc = "eminence") and his followers. Major brings back his defeated rival Easach-tighinn to propose a replacement tax, and they appeal to Cnoc and his mocking crew to help them solve the problem. When they refuse, Major instructs a shaggy wee Shetlander who helps by bookkeeping to reduce the size of the problem by moving the impost from possession of a head to the purchase of commodities. This has such satisfactory features as giving less relief to the poor and rewarding misers and more to the elderly women on whom so much depends. By a triumph of lateral thinking, the Great Rebel decides to replace it with a combination of head tax and property tax, assuming, with the logic one would expect, that the respective unpopularities will cancel each other out - a sort of political homeopathy.

Little Lambeth Pal

Easach-tighinn resurrects the ancient ditty which had radio listeners' feet tapping in the golden days when TV was as rare a minority interest as truffles:

> Everything's free and easy,
> Do as you damn' well pleasy;
> Why don't you make your way there?
> Go there? Stay there?
> Every little Lambeth gal
> With her little Lambeth pal -
> You'll find 'em all
> Doin' the Lambeth Walk.

Easach-tighinn is making a daring reference: it is in Lambeth, an ill-favoured corner of the Vile Morass best known for an archbishop's palace and a resentful and umbrageous population, that the TV John Major first emerges from the Morass into the cold light of day, having left school with nothing to show for it and then applying himself to study to obtain preferment at the bank. The second line is another fine Rabelaisian touch, based on the Abbey of Theleme: "All their life was spent not by laws, statutes or rules, but exercising their own free will and pleasure. They rose out of their beds when they thought good; they did eat, drink, labour. sleep when they had a mind to it, and were disposed for it. None did awake them, none did offer to constrain them to eat. drink or do any thing... In all their rule and strictest tie of their order there was but this one clause to be observed, DO WHAT THOU WILT." One theme common to both *Tales of Tachair* and *Thumping Majority* is that an attempt to take the Thelemite libertarianism seriously leads to a torrent of laws, statutes and rules to impose freedom on those who prefer to do other things, like their duty, their best or what is right.

Frightful things must have happened to him in Lambeth: whenever confronted with the possibility that Cnoc might bring his majority to an end, he cries out: "Oh, yes; oh, yes; go to Lambeth; go to Lambeth and see what's happened there." So far, no episode has shown him with a handbell to match the town crier's formula, but no doubt that time will come. After all, when he expresses pique at being disbelieved, he protests that he has said it month after month after month after month" - a direct echo of Lewis Carroll: "I have told you once, I have told you twice;/ What I tell you three times is true." (the Bellman in *The Hunting of the Snark*). Meanwhile, "doing the Lambeth Walk" has become a synonym for walking away from decisions.

This subtlety links Major/Hyde, unendowed clerk, with Major/Jekyll, great scholar: one commentator on whose refusal to state a preference in respect of Ockham and Godham observes: "This balancing, hesitating and inconclusive judgment is very characteristic of Major's intellect." The old boy also considers that "it becomes not a woman ... to wander far from home" and comments on "the fickle temper of the English, whose delight it is to get a new ruler" - an apposite postscript to seeing off Tachair. He is no democrat, however: "There is nothing more unprofitable than a rebellion of the common people and government at their hands, for they make a general unreasoning overturn of everything; when they have to pass judgment or sentence upon men, it is without discrimination that they do so."

His namesake goes to Huntingdon (once held by Scots) and continues his progress through "the university of life". The old boy was certainly sharp, so it is pure lampoon to make the new one an absent-minded *Comic Cuts* professor. He explains he does not remember humdrum things like details of his schooling and being unwell - a trait used to display not the usual amiable bumbling, but the triple role of tormentor, pitiless wretch and muddier of waters attempted by the weird sisters. He makes the memorable remark: "I don't recall asking them to mount this particular insurrection" in response to appeals to stop the Bush-whacked despot from killing the wives and children of menfolk in revolt. What he has actually said is that if the despot's people depose him, "I for one will not weep for him." No doubt it is little more than a quip, like King Henry's gruff, "Who will rid me of this turbulent priest?" Three literal-minded knights gallop off and kill Thomas a Becket, and thousands of Kurds spring to arms against their oppressor. The difference is that King Henry is penitent about the consequences of his petulant remark.

TV Major surrounds himself with Cambridge graduates (a pretty touch: perhaps graduates of Paris, Glasgow and St Andrews will follow). Some are Initiates of Uillseac branded with the cabalistic letters QC, and call one another "learned". ("Quagmire Cavorter?" Fancifully, it must be said, QC may signify simply "Quintin chattering". The title "learned" is used to justify chattering about everything.) They incline to colourless occupational names like "Baker" and "Clarke" with equally colourless personalities, although there is a second McGregor (Wee or Wet John) who becomes programme controller; and a fellow with the sinister name of War Grave charged with peacefully burying the health service under a mound of accountants.

Much care has been given to establishing his illiteracy, as when he called something a "bogus sham" when clearly he meant a real sham. He has been known to add "ever" after "never" for emphasis, and says that he does not "lay in bed worrying". In a medium where "milestone" and "watershed" are used as synonyms for "landmark", it is not surprising to find his metaphors queer. He recommends "safe havens". Where? In the mountains, hundreds of miles from any harbour. He proposes to "catch a tidal wave of human rights.. We must ride that wave, or be carried along by it." Some rider.

Solecism is infectious. Major talks about a "positive shortage", an innocent enough slip for one professionally concerned with "negative growth", but immediately the plague spreads. A QC from Edinburgh with a decent education, trying to justify the line chosen for a railway, claims that the impact on the environment will be "greatly minimised". Even the lofty Urad, in charge of foreign affairs, whose vulgar name is a holdover from Tachairesque Gaelic punning, calls something "potentially useless".

There is one word that Major and his colleagues eschew: "compulsory", thump though they may. When refugees are compelled to go back home, it is called "involuntary repatriation"; when this is criticised, it is called "mandatory repatriation", as if there were some special licence for it. Early in his elevation, Major aired his views: "I know an awful lot of people who have an awful lot of qualifications and if professors looking in will forgive me, they are totally useless, most of them. They have no common sense at all." Later he confesses he can see no possibility of improvement. "I don't think I'm in the business of changing myself. I don't think that it would look right; I don't think it would be right." At his first festival of adulation Tachair appeared, like Banquo at the feast, applauded to the echo by the assembled devotees. She said nothing, just like Banquo's ghost. Then she went away. Telemajor was spared any thoughts of rugged Russian bears or Hyrcan tigers, and celebrated his own translation to her office with the burning phrase: "I've got it, and I like it, and with your help I'm going to keep it."

Attiring this vulgarian Faustus in the aura of great schoolman is a cruel satire, but no harsher to the historical Major's memory than the barbs of Rabelais, Buchanan (who made obvious puns on Major's name) and Erasmus. My theme in fact derives from Erasmus's *Praise of Folly* (1511): "The best happiness is that which is based on illusion, since it costs least; it is easier to imagine oneself a king than to make oneself a king in reality."

Countless millions while away idle hours identifying with an anti-hero who achieves his ambition - beats the system and becomes its master - by doing nothing at least cost, forgetting as he goes along. The basic idea may be astringent as well as abstruse, but *Tales of Tachair* ran for twelve years to an audience of whom few had the Gaelic. Still, the last word lies with the old Master himself. Commenting on the decision of John, Earl of Carrick, to change his name to Robert on becoming King of Scots in 1390 to avoid the bad cess of the name John, he remarks in quaint scholastic way: "To speak truly, there inheres in a name naught, whether good or evil." The high repute of the Sage of Gleghornie, we must hope, will continue to soar sublime above the trivial inventions of the television age.   **Innis Macbeath**

Donald C Farquhar

SMAA IS THE WEICHT O MAN

                Hingin
             atween the
          lift an the yird
      movin tae the swey o the mune
       caain in the wab o the sin
         smaa is the weicht o man
            takkin the fush
               frae the
                 sea

                Gurly
              the thrang
           o the winter swaw
       frichtit nou the men on the sea
        hingin atween life an daith
         smaa is the weicht o man
            takkin the fush
               frae the
                 sea

               Aichan
              doun tae
          the wattery deep
       doukin in want o a schuil
   soundin doun the sea is tuim the sea is tuim
         smaa is the weicht o man
            takkin the fush
               frae the
                 sea

CHERNOBYL HAIRST

Aicht hunner thousan weans A'm telt
A canna haud the nummer,
are deein sair frae pizzen dreed
the sicht wid mak ye wunner.
A ferlie wis the Nuclear Guid a ferlie sae it wis.
Chernobyl gied the yird the pouer
tae mak it loupin green.
Gied the fowk baith licht an het
an pouer for their darg.
The hairst is in, the yird is deid
the parks are dark an caum.

the flouers on the rodden tree
the bumbees on the gean.
The park's whaur cuddies sned the gress,
the gowan on the grun.
They dwyned awa baith howe an ben
like snaw faas aff a dyke.
The weans is drappin jist the same
like flouers in the win.
Aicht hunner thousan weans A'm telt
A canna haud the nummer.
Aicht hunner thousan weans A'm telt
they winna keek the simmer.

BAIRNS

Craik cries the corbie
for it drapped tae the grun
bluid for the bairns
at has tae be fin.
Sned a new born
frae a beast bi the waa
pike oot a ferlie
then up an awa.

Ferlie cry the bairns
as mither cams in
stappin their mou's
wi bluid frae the bane.
The corbies are crawin
for sunkits sae braw.
Steerless an blin
the bairn at's awa.

BOURTREE

Ma bourtree shaws its winters nou
flouers ay an growthie.
But whiles in the haurder air
ye ken it's humphie-Geordie.
A snag is aff a brekan bou
the tweestin shank a ferlie.
A mousie bydes aroun ma taes
whaur stours they tak a baurley.
The burds at cairry aa ma seed
ilk twal month mak thaim leerie.
Tae spried ma bairns aroun the yird
smaa wunners, och am weary.

STANY GRUN

A find a flouer in stany grun
it raxed mang the wrack.
The peerie dancer that widna dee
it's taes were in a crack.
A blaw its face a gowden smirk
a licht for weary een
an syne the bairns were on their wey
tae find anither hame.

DAFFIN

The flouers nod their daffin wey
for caller wins is fuffin.
Bum-bees bum as shanks they swee
the yowes is shairly lauchin.
Whit fuils is fowk at luik sae saft
wi herts at's slippy duntin
noddin heids in simmer days
wi winter yont the laggin.

BACK-END BIRL

A daurk win steired back-end blades
like a gowden drift o snaw.
It wisna weit bit thair wis stour in the lift.
Ahint the dyke in the deeps o a blade bing
a warm beast biggit a hame.
Wi nichts drawin in an burds fleein south
the lan wis shiftin tae the cauld time,
tae the slawer turn o the year.
Owre nicht heich bens skiffed wi snaw,
bi the morn's licht, emerant.
Owre heid stravaigin cluds rin this wey an yon
tae the back-end birl o the win.
On the brae side a plantin whuspers.
"Whit's daein, whit's daein?"

THE KILL

Cauld it wis,
wi the snaw on the grun.
Twa days auld the faa,
rinnin nou, wi the weit o the win.

The cluds gae breingin by
blinkin out the licht o the sun.
The guns, tattie-bogles strung
on twa cheeks o the wuid.
Streitcht like beads,
Cooried ahint the dyke.

Slaw nou the daith mairch
o the beaters.
This wis the last day, hinner end o the saison.
A chitter gangs thro the wuid,
burds are dour tae flee,
scuttern, rinnin afore the men.
The dunt o a wing as a burd
flees up.
Crack gaes a gun!
The burd hauds for a wee,
then faas like the snaw
saft tae the grun.
Thrie mair tae the lift.
Thrie mair that are taen.
Frae the daw tae the daurk the gemm
gaes on.
Twa breks for the guns
for a lauch an a gless.
Nae breks for the burds.

Twa burds in the gloamin
that's up an awa.
Fower cracks o a gun
at the yin that is fleein,
the ither is doun.
Twa dunts an it's hit,
stertin tae faa.
A whussle at last
caas a stap tae the kill.
Caas doun the guns
frae the heid o the brae.
Caas in the dugs
frae the howe an the burn.
Quait the wuid as the reik
poosks awa.

The win deein doun
tae a souch bi the burn
an the licht o the snaw
shaws the reid o the sun.

Donald C Farquhar

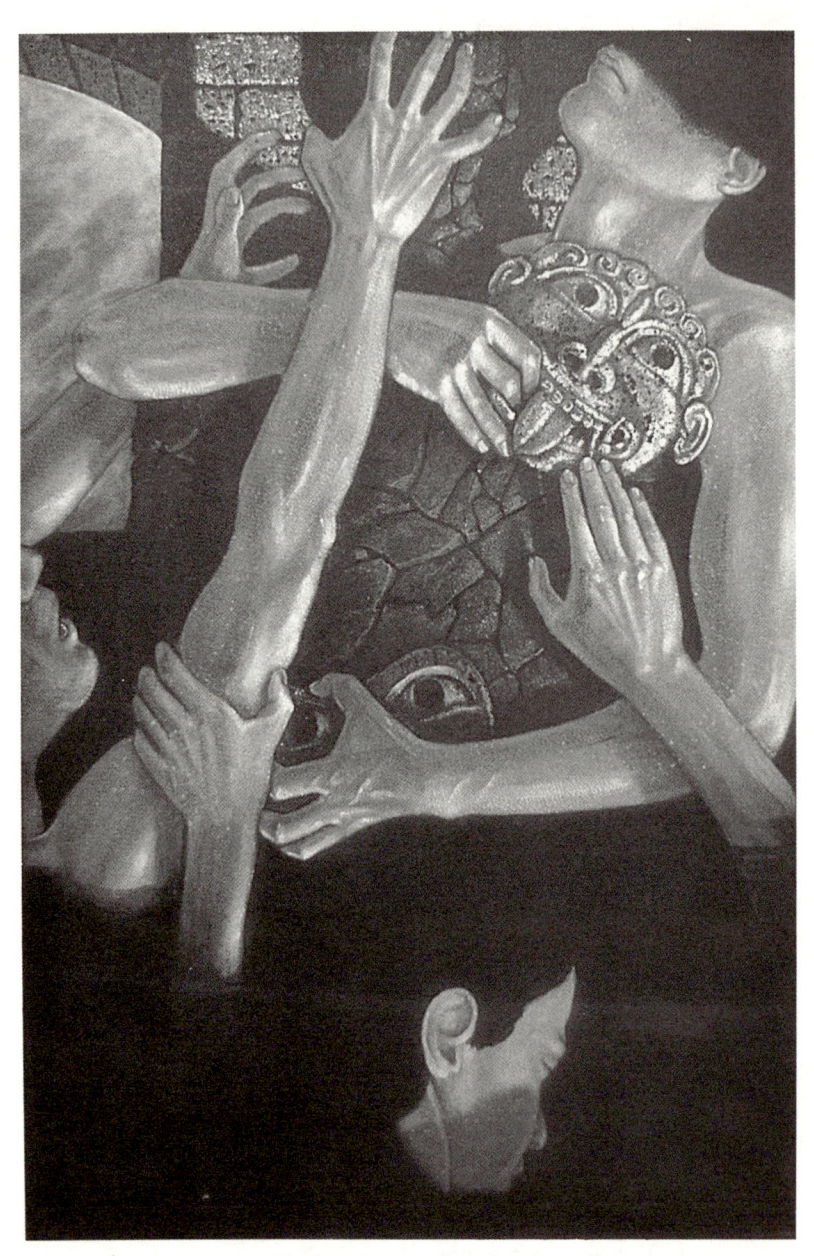

Illustration by Koert Linde

Koert Linde

I was a stone once. My bed was a stone, my blanket a stone. I slept there for centuries and never shed a tear. You, moon, you were my nurse, my sister, and watched over me all through the white night of the ice age. Until the sun slinked back into the sky and woke up a crow, squawking to get out of this impregnable shell.

Iron ore in the brain. A stone between the jaws. A lump of wet clay in the belly. Clouds piled thick between the legs. Smouldering ashes in the grate of the ribs. Icy rivers just below the paper-thin skin. The whole pain-edged world is bound within these soot-stained rags.

You are what is lacking, and what is longed-for: the horizon that always recedes, the void, where creation is still auspicious.

The one who has a horse's head - it is he who made me walk so clumsily. The one who has the claws of an owl - it is he who made me weak and sleepy in the evenings. The one who has the heart of a sheep - he made me cold and hairless like a foetus. No wonder the world is a riddle whose only solution is the world.

But I carry a charter given by the one who has gone from the beginning: a hole in the heart left by the knife-thrust of your word.

You left me with a head emptied of brain and stuffed with linen. You left me with senses sealed with resin and written upon with spells and curses. You left me with bowels deposited in closed jars just beyond my reach. You left me with a penis dried, and preserved in blackest pitch. You left me with arms tied with ribbons, legs bandaged with cloth. You left me an insect flying through the catacombs of what remains of my body. You left me for dead. You've woken me up.

First, I take a broken jug and place it on the soil and pour the best red wine into it - so the earth will drink, and the dead will not be thirsty, and you will listen to my voice. Then, I take a loaf of fresh bread spiced with cloves and cinnamon, and scatter the crumbs out over the river - so that the sea will eat, and the dead will not grow hungry and perish, and you will turn and look at me.

Last, I light a fire, seize a lamb from its mother and sink a knife into its throat. I catch the blood in a wide bowl, lay the sliced meat on a platter, and burn both blood and meat, leaving myself with only a bone to chew - so that heaven will be fragrant, and the dead will send us warning, and you will stand beside me, sharing in this misery.

At the first gate, they wrenched the raven-black cloak from your shoulders.

At the second, they slashed the rope around your pale white wrists.

At the third, they ripped the leaf-green dress from your body.

At the fourth, they tore the silver jewellery from your ears and neck.

At the fifth, they shaved the golden hair from your head and pubis.

At the sixth, they stripped the livid skin from your flesh, and peeled the red flesh from your bones.

Finally, at the seventh gate, they removed the blindfold from your eyes, and slammed shut all the seven doors behind your back.

Thus we meet in this, the darkest chamber of all: two corpses in the precinct of winter, we gaze at each other speechless with love.

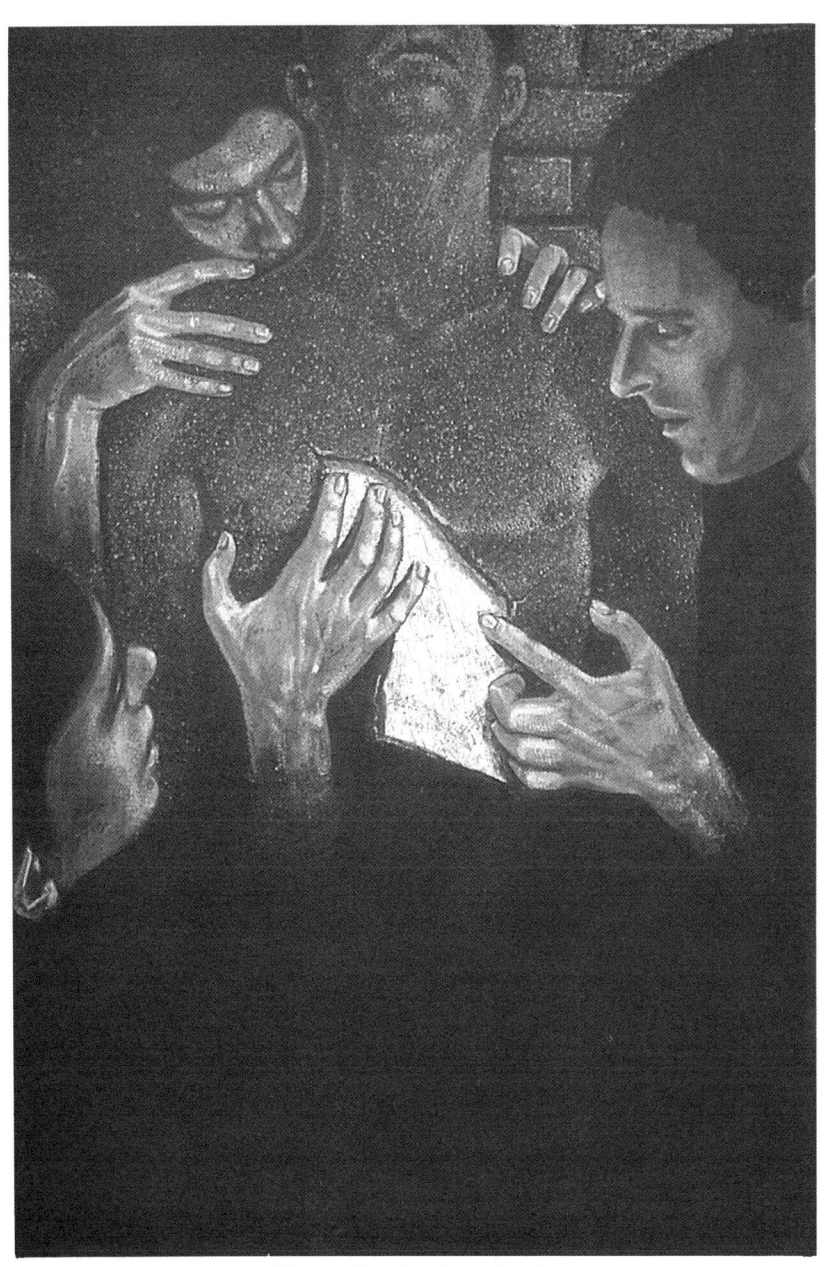

Illustration by Koert Linde

"Let there be light". It was said by the devil. Just as this warren of stars is the work of the devil. And this city of insects, these pastures of idle dreams, all the work of the devil. There is not a single thing in this house of wax that does not bear the mark of his grubby fingers.

And now you appear at the darkest door and cry breathlessly: "Come! There is another world!"

Your face is the tablet of memory. Your eyes are the memory of a garden. Your speech is the garden of forgetfulness. Pass me by, visitor of the spirit, I have no strength.

I saw your face once in the forest. The weight of all the clouds was resting on your head and the roots of the trees were clinging to your feet. Yet you moved lightly among your companions and when I drew closer you were gone. When I saw your face again, many years later, yours was a face in a crowd of similar faces: but the clouds were behind your eyes and the tree roots in your heart, and I recognised you. Now I wait for the day of our third encounter: you may be a ship on the ocean, or a dusty book on a shelf.

Your body was a column of salt. Your speech was a murmur of waves. What matter if you fled as soon as I turned to look? To have seen you once is to remember the beginning is without end.

"Don't leave me here!", I cried when you ran out of the garden weeping, with your clothes torn, and your face smeared with soil; but the gardener held me back, and I watched you slowly disappear across the barren fields, with a red ribbon in your hair, until only the crows circling above your head indicated where you walked.

Koert Linde

Fifth Estate: Four Boards and a Passion
Sandy Neilson

The only sane and logical answer to the proposition "Let's start a new theatre company" is not one that could be safely reproduced in an organ of such refinement and taste as *Chapman*. A desire to work in theatre is a symptom of terminal lunacy, but to compound that with the foolhardy notion of creating a theatrical outlet is to abandon the last shreds of sanity to a future of Lewis Carrollian proportions. Curiouser and curiouser. So the big question is: "Why Fifth Estate?" Particularly in the current financial climate, the motivations must be pretty powerful.

They were. We - Allan Sharpe, Sean Hunter, Paul Ambrose Wright and myself hadn't been having much fun in our various spheres as actor/writer/-director, company manager and designer for quite some time. We wanted to get our teeth into work that stretched and satisfied us. We wanted to work with texts that came off the page with freshness and energy, to use the skills we knew we and others had. So we established Fifth Estate to present to the Scottish audience plays of a high literary standard and produce work across a broad spectrum, irrespective of sources or nationality. Just like that.

We are none of us tyros and we could not say that we didn't know the problems. The main one was finding funding. We decided to deal with that initially and at a stroke, by ignoring it. It seems a Quixotic step but drastic situations sometimes call for absurd responses. To say why we felt constrained to behave in this manner it's perhaps easiest to take a look at the record over the last decade as regards the state of Scottish theatre.

The devolution vote of 1979 and the advent of Thatcherism saw the end of a remarkable period of growth and energy which had created a wide, diverse, and largely autonomous Scottish theatre. There had been, then, reason for writers, directors, designers and actors to stay in and return to Scotland. A tangible sense of excitement was in the air - no longer was Scotland seen as a backwater, but as a developing area in which one felt part of something larger than just the theatrical experience - part of a national movement of regeneration, both political and cultural. Everyone associated with Scottish theatre then had a real sense of purpose and a feeling that their work was important. Miraculously, London had become marginalised.

Then came the twin blows of 1979. The failure of the electorate to grasp what small opportunities the Scotland Bill presented had a profound, almost traumatic effect on the whole theatrical constituency. The steam seemed to go out of the movement - not all at once, but gradually, like a supertanker losing power and coming to a stop over a long distance when only its own momentum kept it going. It might have been possible to restart the engines but Thatcherism's swingeing cuts in public expenditure cut off the fuel supply. Market forces carried the day and it seemed there was nothing could be done about it. The effect on the creative development of theatre in Scotland was devastating: entrenchment became the order of the day - keep your head down, keep your nose clean, and don't make waves.

Today the effects of a decade of 'Safety First' are only too evident. In main houses, energies are channelled into keeping the building visible. The artistic director is no longer the linch-pin of the company: rather it is the administrative element - the general manager, the accountant, fund-raiser, marketing person and bookkeeper who call the shots. It is as though what goes on stage has become incidental - even something of a nuisance - and creativity is being scrapped in favour of balancing the books. Few risks are taken with material and even fewer with new writing.

At the other end of the spectrum are some small-scale companies created in the 70s to massage the unemployment figures and reflecting their origins in issue-based social drama. These hardy touring companies tramp on round halls and community centres, spending much energy merely surviving, sticking to their brand image, synonymous with a particular category of product by which their audiences identify them - and, more significantly, expect of them.

The theatre in 1990 reflected the state of the nation - hard pressed, afraid to innovate, just managing. It has simply stopped being fun. This may sound trivial, but it is, of course, vital. Nobody, let's face it, goes into this business for the money, or if they do, are swiftly disillusioned - it is a hard profession distorted by the glittering prizes awarded to a tiny percentage of its workers. The motivating force has more to do with creative enjoyment, and when the joy goes, the creativity goes with it and it becomes a mere job. Not an easy one either. We were lucky that we found others - writers, directors and actors - crazy enough to want to join us.

Writers are crucial. To date we have mounted two plays by George Rosie. Our first, and his first, *The Blasphemer*, failed to find a home with any of the established companies. It was an immediate critical and popular success. His second, *Carlucco and the Queen of Hearts*, our 1991 Festival production was awarded a *Scotsman* Fringe First, the *Independent* Theatre Award and the *Evening News* National Award. We have been good for each other.

Writers are not always so fortunate. Because of the difficulties experienced by main theatres, the potential to develop new writers is in small scale foundation theatres which precariously lurch from grant to possible grant without foundation of continuity. It is a lottery precluding any form of realistic planning or forward projection. Private sponsorship may be the Tories' Big Idea for arts subsidy, but, for the small scale enterprise it simply doesn't work. If the amount of private subsidy sucked in by 'prestige' companies consequently released the equivalent amount for their public allocation to be passed down the line then the principle might hold a dribble of water - but that's not how it functions. The big fish attract private subsidy as an addition to their public funding, not the small company of relatively unknown origin. Corporate sponsors are not well known for their risk-taking proclivities and cannot understand that 'small scale' merely describes a physical area and not necessarily breadth of vision. A gloomy picture.

Yet we had reason for feeling optimistic when we staged *The Blasphemer*. From the first line it was clearly the kind of play we wanted, witty and literate, a clever, well-made and entertaining piece of work using language with exceptional skill and conviction. It is also great fun. Mounting this play demonstrated to us and our audience what might be done. There is a substantial reservoir of talent in this country, particularly now London has lost its appeal, and, amongst the pedestrian and the polemic, good work is going on - but it needs nurturing and encouragement. It is within this context that Fifth Estate has developed its policy.

The company unashamedly embraces the criterion of 'literary merit' in the choice of material: plays deserving a life long after their first production. Whilst we have an emotional commitment to new work from Scotland we do not rule out previously-performed material or plays from other countries or cultures we feel attention should be drawn to. Our second production, and the play's world premiere was We, Charles XII by Bernard da Costa, translated from the French by Allan Sharpe. As Joyce MacMillan wrote in *The Guardian* "The script is full of ideas and eloquent to a fault." "full of striking language, imagery and symbolism" said Raymond Ross in the *Evening News*. The production was praised for strong performances and superb design. It went on to full production in Paris in October 1991.

Having found such material we are resolved that lack of finance will not be a barrier to production. If the merit is there, we will find a way of producing it. We believe that literary theatre is important for the continuity and development of our national theatrical culture and that people like - and will pay to see - good, well-made plays. This belief has been amply vindicated by our first three productions, which were sell-outs night after night. And so we are looking for plays of like calibre. Plays that deal with the perennial as opposed to the ephemeral, plays that bring metaphor back into the theatre and that deal with the individual in terms of the human condition. Plays which are enjoyable for being intellectually rigorous.

Apart from providing an outlet for writers contemplating work of this nature, encouraging them to be more expansive in approach and subject matter, by test-running these plays, even to limited audiences, we effectively remove the risk to main houses of future programming, enabling second productions and acceptance into the long term repertoire of Scottish theatre - a problem dogging the development of new work for many years.

We admit freely that our own judgment will determine what we believe to be work of high literary merit and that we run the risk of having our judgement questioned - nay ridiculed. We will not relinquish the right to fail and we have no intention of playing safe. We feel the time is right for these policies, sensing the need to bring excitement and challenge back to the top of the agenda. Difficult plays give us difficult problems to solve; and problem-solving stimulates the creative juices and keeps our interest alive.

We have a realistic approach to funding. We are now completing our first year of operation and cannot expect revenue funding immediately. Although doing everything to attract funding we are determined that lack of financial resources will neither limit our output nor lower our self-imposed standards. A return to Grotowski's Poor Theatre or Peter Brook's Empty Space may be no bad thing to begin with. The old concept of theatre being possible with four boards and a passion still encapsulates the essential elements that lie at the roots of real theatre. If the space is filled with imagination, vision and, most importantly, freedom, then the resulting work will have satisfying

*Robin Thomson and Muriel Romanes in **We, Charles XII** by Bernard de Costa,
Fifth Estate, Netherbow, Edinburgh 1991*

substance - a partnership of writers, actors, designers and directors working together with a common cause, provoked by the simple desire to do it and not solely motivated by the promise of a pay cheque - true creativity.

Contrary to received wisdom, there is no shortage of the sort of plays we are looking for. In our first year we will have produced five major projects out of an overall budget of £9,500 and intend to maintain as high a turnover of material as possible. Both impetus and continuity are important factors in any enterprise of this nature. In doing so, we expect to build a creative infrastructure of theatre workers (even within the financial constrictions of profit-sharing). Since being founded on insecurity is built into our thinking we can, paradoxically, plan ahead, setting our own timetables and tempo. We are mounting a production of *Buchan of Tweedsmuir* by Trevor Royle for the Borders Festival, while rehearsing *Carlucco and the Queen of Hearts* for transfer to Hampstead Theatre Club and *The Archive Of Countess D* by Alexis Aputchtine to open in November at the Netherbow Theatre. The Netherbow has given us a much-needed base for our first productions and we share a corner of an office with the Scottish Society of Playwrights though we have to do administration in our 'spare' time. We have learned as a consequence of success that adminstrators these days cannot be amateur - a problem we have to address.

Our plans for next year include neglected plays by Joan Ure and the first revival of Donald Campbell's *The Jesuit*. For the Festival we have one excellent certainty and some intriguing possibilities in the wings. Watch this space. Our core team will remain substantially the same with the addition of two fine Scottish actors who want to move into directing, each currently assistant-directing in preparation for a solo stint. That they, and the rest of the company of experienced, often senior actors, are willing to 'donate' their work for a share of what small profit may accrue from the run speaks volumes for the attractions of working with our chosen texts.

The dedication and commitment of practitioners supplies the subsidy without which ticket prices would work out at £25 per seat. Company members have to earn their livings elsewhere while retaining a commitment to Fifth Estate. This necessitates a large company core but secures a variety of creative input and cross-fertilisation that will make the dangerous cul-de-sac of stylistic stagnation unlikely. There will be no 'house style'; rather each play will receive a fresh approach to the individual demands it makes of the company with the consequent enrichment of both opportunity and experience. We exist to stimulate both audience and the people who work with us - we aim to bring adventure, challenge, excitement and, above all, joy back into the Scottish theatrical experience. From that we all benefit.

We have not set ourselves up in opposition to any other theatre company or organsation. We believe that the work of every theatre is a valid contribution to our culture. But as long as the current funding structure militates against risk, adventure and progress, there is little hope for the future of indigenous theatre in Scotland - indeed there is little future for writers, actors, technicians, directors and designers, or audiences - or for their great-great-grandchildren. And we will all be the poorer for that.

Sandy Neilson, for Fifth Estate

Maureen Macnaughtan

ROOTS

Follow, follow, feel the old need,
kindle a new fire.
Before the routes grow wilder
forget the charred pretenders,
stem this grinding disease
the flood and the briar.

Hurry, follow, make your escape
then stretch the wishing net.

From every part of the globe
nostalgia longs for recognition.
Down in the city square
drums fill the silence
of a well-established tradition.

The recruiters are round again
shedding sincerity like a skin
choosing between the mob.
Kitchener widened the track,
no glossy video for him
just the old white heather
and a one-way-ticket back.

They'll join that granite list.
Oh the fighting Scot
against all the evidence
until his dying day -
he's more volatile in war
than learning how to heal
a fester of complacency.

WINTER SMOKE

Awake, and restore the poppies
let the masses mow the lawn.
Where are the blood-lust Vikings
to torch this frozen parade?
Proud Edward would lie easy
in the welcome that rattles
behind satellite cups.

Ever anxious to blame the enemy
ice-years have kept Snow-White
horizontal in electric blankets.
Jack Frost the heat has gone,

under this crisp tablecloth
a chintzy highland massacre
waits to dust the summer shingle.

Stay in your fur-boots lady
the Auld Alliance is continental,
Stewart and Saxe-Coburg
have twinned to meet the demand.
Sir Walter auctions the casket-letters,
we are more firmly Anglicised
than the stately oaks of England.

MOCH

In the shap chyce wis gey antrin
Bein in the daurk,
I liftit the neist globe.
Sinsyne ye've been
Fair set on yir daith.
That shade wis richt intendit
Tae haud aff yir deid-thraws.
Aye, in maist honest wars
Leevin's no fur troke.
Loanins can be riddened
An the clachan ha's cloured.

This lang, nicht draws on
An aye ye pass an pass again
While ma daurk flichterin's
Tyauve tae faa on this leaf.
Awa! Tak yir rampagin ithergates!
The maist laichsome pairt o me
His a dwynin hankerin
Tae haud the buik agee.
Noo that yir flufferins are past
I'll show ye hoo tae thole,
Birslin, in slaw slaw grees.

TORII'S GIFT

(Based on a Kabuki Play)

You gave me a token, a piece of moon madness
Which waits like a child for the blessing to come.

All of our hopes were carved from a promise,
whatever there was he nursed into flame.

They beg us to part, to save them the sorrow
so my cheeks can drown in an ocean of tears.

Torii, love is a blossom that chooses the orchard,
it makes no condition, yet I hold your song.

Years before the pledge my heart was uncertain,
I bowed to the trap thinking wisdom would soothe.

Love came like a conqueror, to ride in triumph,
to crush my dreams and fever my senses.

We were not thieves for passion steals nothing
I never wanted this tortured samisen.

His heart found excuses - in one freezing moment
your precious gift took the mountain from me.

When we first met the sun was shadowed,
just to hold him caused the sweetest of pain.

You left us guilt, a victory to choke on,
a serpent ripped from a madman's throat.

I leave you a gift, the bright juice of honour,
may the moon hide her face till the stars forget.

LEDA

Do not dream, my child
such doors are easily closed.
Let the taste of hunger
strengthen and reverberate.

Some summer evening
when the surface of the pool
is moused into a ripple,
you'll hear the owl crunch
on a speck of shrieking life.

Once I went quivering,
to snatch without restraint
all the savage passion
that no beak could hold.

Rise and stand by the water's edge
look down on your own reflection,
what is in our hearts
can shame the fires of hell
and make the moon transparent.

Come, Apollo cannot warm us.
His crown was lost
when the blood of emotion
honoured such a birth.

How slow the fruit ripens
yet the blaze has eagle-wings.
My soul weeps for thee,
already that terrible charm
echoes in your smile.

Maureen Macnaughtan

Gael Turnbull

IN THE IONIAN

Hand scarcely on tiller, a light breeze
abeam, starboard tack, leaving harbour,
bearing south west in the early sun
until, resolving out of haze, a headland
wine dark on the horizon, named
and famed in words, transfixing history,
where one displaced by war, misfortune,
yearned to return, so we, retracing,
laying a course to find a landfall

and holding course, beneath port bow,
breakers out from beyond a cliff base,
tightening sail, as a squall unnoticed
from open sea to west heels us over
with heavy swell, the breakers nearer,
going about, almost not, then clearing
eye of the wind, boat trembling forward
through blood dark crests with marbled foam,
weight straining against the tiller.

WITH HOMAGE TO THAT CRITIC

who advised it was of great importance
for all kinds of sake, in these days
of book deluge, to keep out of the salt
swamps of literature and live
on your own rocky island with a lake
and a spring on it, though why so many
should have a pure taste in words yet
false taste in art was a phenomenon
which puzzled not a little;

and of the moderns, to keep to Z -,
while Y -'s "X -" was, so far as he knew,
the greatest the century had produced
but to cast aside W - as shallow and
to give up V -, if not able, as you would

sea bathing until strong enough, and never
to read bad poems or write poetry yourself,
there being perhaps rather too much
than too little in the world already.

IMPELLINGS

As a dunnock, scarcely fledged,
strayed from heed of parents,
perched on an upper ledge, quivers
and flares its wings, tensed and eager
to be loosed, then projects itself
out exulting upon the air
where a sparrowhawk registers, locks
upon, impelled also and by desire,
curving in flight to meet

so, winged and finned, lifting
from their cradles, balanced on flame,
a plume following, stately, the emblems
of device, yearning on course, ascend
through cloud beyond our sight
to make revelation in a ripple
of brightness, the sound following
only after pause, as if an echo
returning from the unheard.

THAT WIND

"For the wind blaws whaur it will
and ye hear the souch o it ... "
at interval and by continuance
bringing rain, drought, snow, haar
then clear sky and by night, frost
with stars, as it crests and trembles
the spindrift blaa: sheep's wool
snagged on whin, briar, dyke,
wavering evidences that cling

in traces to be gathered, carded,
spun, rewoven by such as need -
packmen, drovers, vagrant singers,
disbanded men from far-off wars -
by contrivance patching garments,
shelter against that wind, who track,
are driven, those upland roads
"but whaur it is comin frae
and whaur it is gaein til . . ."

Gael Turnbull

REVIEWS

A SPECTRUM OF GAELIC WRITING

An Aghaidh Na Siorraidheachd: Eight Gaelic Poets ed Christopher Whyte, Polygon, £9.95; *Bardachd Na Roinn-eorpa An Gaidhlig*, ed Ruaraidh MacThomais, Gairm, £7.50; *Gaelic and Scots in Harmony*, ed Derick S Thomson, Dept of Gaelic, Glasgow University, £9; *Gaelic and Scotland*, ed William Gillies, EUP, £29.95; *Gaelic - A Past and Future Prospect*, Kenneth MacKinnon, Saltire Society, £7.95; *Coinneach Odhar*, Domhnall Iain MacIomhair, Gairm, £5.40

In her foreword Meg Bateman points to the origins of her poetic career in family misfortune and personal loss. A fresh eye on those eternal themes, love and death, appears in her poetry. She has a talent for condensed poetic biography in well-constructed verses of which *'A chionn's gu robh mi measail air'* ('Because I was so fond of him') and *'Bha mi gad chaineadh'* (I was reviling you) are fine examples. *'Alba fo Dhimeas'* ('Scotland Despised') neatly expresses the refusal of Scots to see the best in their heritage, a recurring theme in the poems in this anthology.

Myles Campbell couples love with a despair at poetic silence in *'Duilleagan'* ('Leaves'): "The world around full of jewels/ and my dumbness shouting that the pen was useless". His exasperation at Scotland's cultural subjection (and ignorance) frequently shows through, as does his sadness at the changes of the island where he now lives. The four lines of *'An Clamhan'* ('The Buzzard') contain much: "Mull of the spacious moors/ and the deserted townships;/ the buzzard wakeful in his kingdom/ listening to the oral tradition of the wind". Anne Frater shows a similar concern for Scottish dodging of cultural responsibility in *'Ar Cànan s ar Clò'*, *'Smuain'* and *'Lit' gun Shalain'*. *'An Adharc'* ('The Horn') is a fine parable of that condition we have been in too long. *'Geamradh'* ('Winter'), *'Bàs na h-Eala'* ('The Death of the Swan') are gentler in tone, but still a deep-seated regret for things lost.

Refusal to modernise Gaelic lexis is not for Fearghas MacFhionnlaigh who borrows deliberately almost as if he were (quite properly) wagging Gaelic's modern European existence under the reader's nose. This technique works well enough, after the inital shock. He says he is a Christian and a Calvinist and in *'Marbhrann'* ('Epitaph') there is the flavour of a strongly-worded sermon in such lines as *"mhùchadh thu le diobhairt do ghlormhiann fèin"* ("you choked on the vomit of your own vanity") There is an almost apocalyptic flavour to many of these poems.

Aonghas Macneacail's work shows concern with language in poems like *'an tùr caillte'* and less directly in others. Macneacail is an admirer of Carlos Williams and Japanese verse techniques. This shows in a fondness for short, almost gnomic verses as in *'oran luaidh'*, a long poem in short couplets. *'oideachadh ceart'* ('a proper schooling') is less tight and deals with historical episodes welded into a stark narrative on the condition of the Gael. Catriona Montgomery does not dodge issues but writes with commendable bluntness. Her strength is in tough, satirical verse with humane overtones: in *'Roag 2000 AD'* the privileged decadence of incomers contrasts with the struggle of displaced crofters; the anglicised laird is taken apart in *'Aoir'*. *'Obair-Grèis'* casts a sardonic eye on puritanical self-righteousness.

If one looked only at the translations of Christopher Whyte's poems, unaware that the originals were in Gaelic, one would know this was modern European poetry but (apart from place names) find difficulty in pinpointing its provenance. Like MacFionnlaigh, he is more concerned with ideas than location. *'Anns an Ròimh'* contrasts sophisticated chatter about a ghastly outrage in Beirut with a woman's simple delight in the arrival of swallows. The scratched Scot in him turns somewhat theological in *'Rex Tenebrarum'*.

The quality the Welsh call *hiraeth* - a nostalgic yearning for vanished things (not antiquarian sentimentality) comes over strongly in the work of Mary Montgomery. There are, by contrast, a number of salty poems which are bitterly satirical. In *'Na Sassannaich'* she is far from mealy-mouthed: "nothing if not practical/ old chap, dear sir and dame". The bitterness is scalding: almost a modern echo of the *brosnachadh* addressed to Argyll in 1513. She gives a thrashing to absentee landlords in 'If I had an Island'. In all these poets there is skill, eloquence, concern: a strength and lack of posturing.

Since *Bardachd na Roinn-Eòrpa* prints the original poems before the Gaelic settings, an English translation would have been too much to ask for. There are, after all, twenty-five translators and upwards of fivescore poems. There are translations of Breton, Irish, Scots, English, Welsh, Croatian, Dutch, German, Italian, Finnish, French, Greek, Latin, Norwegian, Polish, Maltese, Russian, Spanish, Galician, Ukrainian and Hungarian. One cannot fail to be impressed by the expert, literate transcreations in this relatively inexpensive book. Not many anthologies even in English have a cultural spectrum stretching from ancient Greece to modern Europe. One is doubly surprised, then. to discover in the foreword that The European City of Culture refused to take an interest in it claiming that it was not sufficiently relevant to Glasgow, a city with more Gaelic speakers than any in Scotland (and a book edited by a Professor of Celtic in Glasgow University!)

Derick Thomson edits also the proceedings of the Second International Conference on the Languages of Scotland. *Gaelic and Scots in Harmony* - not only a title but a state of affairs devoutly to be wished by all with our linguistic well-being at heart. This book of scholarship will also attract the general reader interested in Scottish language, literature and social history. There are essays on kin-based society (John Bannerman), Gaelic and Scots place names (W F H Nicolaisen), placenames of Lewis (Richard Cox), Scots and Gaelic domestic lexis (Ian Quick), language in Scottish poems (Helena Shire), the origin of the word 'tartan' (Alan Bruford), dialect developments (Donald MacAulay), Ulster-Scottish relationships (A J Hughes), the sources of Alexander MacDonald's poetry (Derick Thomson), George Campbell Hay's attitudes to nationalism (Christopher Whyte), a comparison of the poetry of Douglas Young and Sorley MacLean (Derick McClure), the poetry of Iain Crichton Smith (Douglas Gifford) and the state of Gaelic now (Kenneth MacKinnon).

From the other end of the Antonine Wall comes *Gaelic and Scotland* a collection of essays on Gaelic literature and history edited by William Gillies, chair of Celtic Studies in the University of Edinburgh. Again, the writings of scholars will surely interest the ordinary reader. William Gillies writes of the study of Gaelic as a branch of higher learning and the sheer *value* of Gaelic as a major part of Scottish cultural consciousness. Catherine Dunn and Boyd Robertson describe Gaelic in primary and secondary education. John Murray writes of education within the Gaelic community and defines it as the place where "the dogs are not bilingual!" - a neat phrase. There are articles both in English and Gaelic. In his essay, John MacInnes describes the Lowlands as seen by the Highlander. It may surprise some that Gaelic speakers in Arran described the entire stretch of coastline from Galloway to Ayrshire as part of the Gaeltachd. And, tells Donald Meek, Alexander Montgomery, the Ayrshire poet (1540-1611?) was a *native* Gaelic speaker from the Gaelic-speaking county of Ayr. It is refreshing to see these facts in print. That Gaelic was commonly spoken in areas now described as Lowland is extensively covered by Charles Withers.

Ronald Black's interesting account of Gaelic manuscripts gives a detailed list of where they are to be found. Kenneth MacDonald, again in Gaelic, writes on the *marbhrannan soisgeulach* - the religious elegies, with extensive quotations from them. Another Gaelic essay, by Donald Archie MacDonald, treats of the cultural link between the Gaels of Ireland and Scotland in their common heritage of story-telling. Naive ideas on the Scottish linguistic heritage will be shattered by a reading of G W S Barrow's account of 'The Lost Gaidhealtachd of Mediaeval Scotland'. There is an essay on the dynamics of a renaissance in Gaelic literature by Donald John Macleod.

Kenneth MacKinnon's book is a history of Gaelic language in Scotland from early times to the present. Possibly a more relaxed introduction to the subject than the two above, there are Gaelic quotations but always with English translation. There is an account of Gaelic cultural life; how a language once common to most Scots, Lowland and Highland, became a cause of contention - *mi-rùn mòr nan Gall* - and the separation of speech-groups into Gaelic and the tongue known as Scots. 'Strategies for Survival', the last chapter, is interesting both for factual information, and for the optimistic feel of the writing: "almost every parish within the 'Highland Line' still has surviving Gaelic speakers".

Claims about the Brahan Seer are given scholarly scrutiny in a paper by William Matheson. *Coinneach Odhar*, written at a more popular level, is a fairly detailed account, listing sayings attributed to the prophet and speculating on their origins. Under a statement that "Ferintosh Kirk, full of people, will collapse when a magpie nests three years in succession in the wall", Iain MacIomhair comments that probably magpies have so nested, but the second part of the prophecy has not yet been fulfilled. Opinions about vaticination vary from outright scepticism to uncritical acceptance with the rest swithering somewhere between. Nevertheless, an interesting and enjoyable book. As MacIomhair says in the introduction, "the reader ... can make up his own mind about any question that may arise".

These six books embrace the whole spectrum of writing in Gaelic. Their appearance is a triumph of spirit over adversity. The shameful truth is that Scotland is full of those who wish to kick the older tongues of our native literature into the yawning gulf of their own ignorance, when, as these books show, Gaelic (and Scots), far from dead, will be with us into next century and beyond.

This review is written as Sorley MacLean approaches his 80th birthday, a poet of international stature who, despite his expertise in English, deliberately chose to write in his native tongue. There are others, less well-known, who have chosen likewise. Yet in Scotland still many accredited pundits of Scottish literature make no visible effort to understand that literature through the tongues in which it is written. That, however, is no fault of the writers listed above.

William Neill

LEXICOGRAPHY'S LEADING EDGE

The Scots Thesaurus, ed Iseabail Macleod, and others, Aberdeen University Press, £18.50

We owe this fascinating book to two circumstances: first, that the distinctive vocabulary of Scots is not only amazingly rich and diverse but intimately associated with the traditional culture and life-habits of the Scottish people; and second, that dictionary-making in Scotland represents theoretical and methodological lexicography at its leading edge. Not even the skill and dedication of the Dictionaries' absurdly small, impoverished research and production teams could have produced the *Concise Scots Dictionary*, the *Pocket Scots Dictionary*, and now the *Thesaurus* - unless in a timespan of decades rather than years - without the advanced techniques of computer-assisted lexicography, in the development of which the Dictionary staff themselves, notably A J Aitken, have been pioneers.

As Alexander Fenton says in his Introduction: "The *Thesaurus* entries represent the distilled outcome of decades of basic research." Indeed they do: the *Thesaurus* is a re-working of the *CSD*, itself an abridgement, and an updating of the *SND* and *DOST*, begun in 1925. The same data has also given us the *PSD*, and more spin-offs are planned. The debt of gratitude we owe to those preservers of cultural heritage - first to David Murison and Jack Aitken, and latterly Harry Watson, Iseabail Macleod, Mairi Robinson, Pauline Cairns, Marace Dareau, Caroline Macafee, Ruth Martin, Lorna Pike and Patricia Wilson - notice anything?? - is such that in a nation worth the name all would now have life peerages at least.

Entries are arranged thematically into fifteen main sections of varying size: "Birds, wild animals, invertebrates", "Water, sea, ships", "Food and drink", "War, fighting, violence" etc. Each has sub-headings: under "Emotions, character, social behaviour" (the biggest section of over 100 pages) we find among "intelligence", "stupidity", "mockery", "thrift, miserliness, avarice", "spendthrifts, spongers" (the second of these last two sections is smaller than the first: because misers are commoner in Scotland? or because, being more disliked, they evoke a bigger selection of derogatory words: *dring, glamsach, grippie, hooky, knapper-knytlych, slughan*?), "gratuitous abuse" and "endearments" (again more of the former than the latter, and the fact that *ratton* and *taid* are pressed into service as endearments might suggest a real paucity of Scots words in this category; but if we eliminate the insult terms for which the source is Dunbar or his flyting partner Kennedy, the imbalance is less). Who will say again that the Scots are not prone to emotional excesses afer finding, under "Strong emotion", well over thirty words suggesting great excitement or agitation, such as *dirdum, feerish, flichter, jabble, panshine* and *yagiment*? What becomes of the myth of the inarticulate Scot when over two pages are taken up with words for "Chitchat", and as much again for "Nosiness, slander"? As a demonstration of the editors' ingenuity in classification, and for sheer fun, "Emotions, character, behaviour" forms the climax of the volume.

Every aspect of Scottish life is treated. In the section on "Farming", we are taken through the yearly cycle of activities from ploughing to harvest, we see over the buildings and the dykes (*clap dyke, consumption dyke, face dyke, fail dyke, Galloway dyke, swear dyke*), we meet farm personnel (*pafflers, pendiclers, grund officers, gaudsmen* and *orra men*). The sections on sea and freshwater fishing, sub-sections of "Water, sea, ships", demonstrate the specialisation of these crafts by words for entities as precisely defined as "one of a row of cords attaching the meshwork to the headrope of a fishing net" (*noozle*) and "a device consisting of three hooks lashed together and fastened to a weighted string" (*paparap*).

In the areas of national institutions, Church, education and law, we find abundant confirmation of their distinctiveness. The Kirk, both pre- and post-Reformation, is treated in several sub-sections; and among the wealth of information about its practices we also find entertaining and revelatory details: much could be deduced about traditional Scottish attitudes from such entries as *paper minister, privy censures, gallopin Tam* and *whistlin Sunday*. Schools and universities have sub-sections under the same heading: there are many words for truancy and tawses, but more interesting are the references to nicknames, traditions and customs associated with individual seats of learning, and parish schools with their *penny bookies, lockerstraes, coolin stanes* and *wheeky-whacky days*. The law is the most extensively treated of all, with a fifty-page section in which the courts and their officers, laws of commerce and property, crimes and punishments, and much else, are presented in fine detail.

"Nothing as nationally comprehensive as the *Thesaurus* has appeared before, in Britain or in any other country," Fenton observes. This is true; and in the *Thesaurus* we have a record of our long-enduring and highly individual national culture which should make a major contribution to keeping at least the memory of that culture alive. All readers, from the learned professor to the casual browser, will find here something to arouse both their interest and, if their souls are not wholly dead, their patriotic pride.

Derrick McClure

WOMEN'S LITERATURE

Soviet Women Writing: 15 Short Stories, int I Grekova, John Murray £14.95; *Feeling Restless: Australian Women's Short Stories 1940-69*, ed Connie Burns, Marygai McNamara, William Collins, £10.95; *Sleeping with Monsters: Conversations with Scottish and Irish Women Poets*, ed Rebecca Wilson, Polygon, £8.95; *Night Geometry and the Garscadden Trains*, A L Kennedy, Polygon, £7.95; *The Virtues, the Vices and all the Passions*, Anita Phillips, Polygon, £7.95

Two collections of short stories by women, one from the Soviet Union and one from Australia, highlight the contrasts between the two cultures, but, more poignantly, re-emphasise without cliche that the more individual an account, the more it draws attention to a common identity. These women writers make the paradox very clear: through what we share we discover that each of us is unique. In the best of each collection it is not the foreign-ness that matters, but the possibility of recognition.

Soviet Women Writing: 15 Short Stories includes stories dating back to 1942, many of which could not be published until the recent relaxation of censorship. Lidia Ginzburg's 'Siege of Leningrad' tackles the horror of the siege in a surreal account of the unnamed protagonist's inner state. The outer world has become the dream; the inner is paramount, delineated with a stylistic precision that even in translation suggests the legacy of Dostoevsky. I Grekova's 'Masters of their own Lives' deals with the similar theme of the individual as overwhelmed by history as dwarfed by the vast scale of the USSR itself. The Estonian stories contrast with the Russian in this respect, prophetically it now seems. 'The Cave' by Mari Saat, exploits the pathetic fallacy by using the natural world to mirror a boy's awakening eroticism, causing nature to waive its laws in the face of the demands of an individual consciousness.

The Australian stories share with their Soviet counterparts an awareness of the untamed vastness of the land itself, showing a basic similarity of environment nurturing two contrasting cultures. *Feeling Restless* overlaps in time with the Soviet stories. The Australian book is a re-issue of stories published at a period believed to have been barren in terms of literature. The editors have succeeded admirably in disproving this notion. Although the Soviet book begins with a token assertion of women's rights under the Soviet system, whereas the Australian editors felt no need to set the fiction in a political context, the images of women's lives are remarkable in their exposure of such universal common ground.

The first story, 'Mrs James Greene', set in the Indian Mutiny, is a gripping account of one white woman's survival presents in a different historical and geographical location questions of class, culture and race, raised many times in their contemporary Australian context. Mary Durak's 'The Double Track' focusses upon young Simeon's philosophical acceptance of two cultures, two creeds; Katherine Susannah Pritchard's deceptively straightforward 'Marlene' makes a sudden shift in point of view which exposes the criminal simplicity of imperialism in contrast with the unsuspected wisdom of the dispossessed. The stark portrayal of women's lives in stories like 'Full Cycle', by Lyndall Haddow, about an Italian wife forced into drudgery on an outback farm, is uncannily like Soviet images. Tamara in Viktoria Tokareva's 'Five Figures on a Pedestal' makes a futile break from a similar slavery, her concluding line equally fitting for the Australian story - "Even the earth had its treadmill."

So is the reality of our own lives very different? Turning from foreign fiction to our own reality, Rebecca Wilson's *Sleeping with Monsters* comprises interviews with twenty-two poets, discussing their lives, the effects of nationality, culture and gender on their work, and, most interestingly perhaps, the way they perceive their work.

Perhaps the interview technique is bound to contain seeds of disappointment, but Wilson does it well. Her transcriptions are lively, readable and informative. However, the highlights of the book are the poems themselves. After all, these women *are* poets. They can express themselves in the demanding and concentrated medium of poetry, and one cannot help wondering how necessary it is to hear more. There is an uneasiness in focussing upon the poet as personality rather than on the poetry itself. It is the work that tells us most about who these writers are. Jackie Kay's 'We are Not All Sisters Under the Same Moon' is an affirmation of self and identity that stands without any supporting conversation:

> For I am not only a strong woman
> with a Scorpio rising I am
> not about to dance with daffodils
> every day making putty out of my wishes
> to shape my future needs. I have no
>
> definite tomorrow only a longing that
> I will write to pick out lights
> that cast curious shadows in the dark.

Some poets in this collection are well published; nearly half have published collections of their own, several since Wilson collected her interviews. Others are almost unavailable elsewhere. Certainly the book draws attention to the fact that there is plenty of material available for an anthology. And the interviews are intriguing.

Possibly transcribed conversations cannot avoid an air of breathlessness, but, when juxtaposed with the Soviet and Australian stories, these accounts of real lives reiterate the same points: women's lives are full of what the Soviets call "byt", a word signifing the endless, unappreciated busy-ness of women's lives and work. They reflect also their time, place and culture, a commonality and an individuality that informs their work.

Two Scottish fiction writers to emerge since Rebecca Wilson did her interviews between 1986 and 1988 are Alison Kennedy and Anita Phillips, who have both recently published first books with Polygon. Kennedy's *Night Geometry and the Garscadden Trains* is a welcome collection of short stories nearly all of which are published separately elsewhere. Kennedy's sparse style, with a singular dearth of adjectives and genius for understated irony, gives her work a sense of disciplined intensity. The twists at the end of 'Tea and Biscuits' and 'The Moving House' work, not because the subject matter is original - Kennedy tends to be too topical for that - but because the narration of the story shocks by its lack of exclamation; a point of view invoking a cool horror that should provoke a reaction from the most exhausted social conscience.

The stories range from Glasgow to a South American mission; one spot we never reach is Garscadden. Indeed, the title story might be a paradigm of Kennedy's method. The Garscadden train nearly kills Duncan, one of several unbearable spouses in the book; and we are left with no destination at all, but a conclusion which refuses to be conclusive: "We live small lives, easily lost in foreign droughts, or famines; the occasional incendiary accident, or a wall of pale faces, crushed against grillwork, one Saturday afternoon in spring. This is not enough." For Kennedy's characters there is never enough. The anger remains implicit, controlled by a precise style and form which shape her stories with peculiar power.

Anita Phillips' *The Virtues, the Vices and all the Passions* uses the 17th century emblem book *Iconologie* as the framework of the novella. The overt use of source is unusual, and the reproduction of the emblems is a major attraction. Whether the story of Vira and Fell's affair sustains its imagery is questionable; it may be too slight for such symbolic superstructure. The final resolution lies not within the story, but in a discussion of the meaning of iconography. Meaning is shown to be, like the story itself, elusive and insubstantial. As Vira remarks: "You're left wondering what on earth an olive branch means when set next to a dead rabbit and an open compass." And perhaps, also, wondering how much it really matters.

Margaret Elphinstone

KEEN ADVENTURES

Easy Money? A True Story of Crime and Punishment, Boyd Keen, Canongate, £14.95; *Our Lady of the Pickpockets*, Dilys Rose, Secker & Warburg, £12.95; *Gay Hunter*, Lewis Grassic Gibbon, Polygon Cosmos (1989); *Blooding Mister Naylor*, Chris Boyce, Dog & Bone, £5

Boyd Keen is a people's writer. The literary elite perhaps wouldn't like it, but for the mass of humanity *Easy Money?* is a work of 'life significance'. I sent Boyd's poems from prison to Joy Hendry back in 1985, as Boyd was desperately looking for honest critique, recognition, and a chance to publish before his book had begun - before he had the confidence to think he could write it. The poetry was acknowledged with the comment that it needed a little work, so would he like to rewrite it. Boyd was incensed. (So incensed that the "honest critique" was not responded to - the Ed) The poems never got published in *Chapman*, although several won awards (Koestler Awards) and were aired on Radio Scotland.

This matters little now: Boyd Keen has hit the big time that his bizarre drug-smuggling adventure never did. *Easy Money?* is an autobiographical epic: six years of an ageing seaman's life gone wrong, told in a raconteur style that reads like a yarn spun over a few hundred pints when you're so rivetted by the stories that you can't move.

Boyd Keen is a West Coast "sea captain" who has spent his life on ships and boats, and when offered a chance to earn 'easy money' late in life, took the gamble, got the dope, and ended up doing five years in four of Scotland's most notorious prisons, at the ripe old age of 60! Such tales of maniacal adventure could never be invented. The old murder-mystery style of weaving past and present events together works like a film script in a book of fat pages and no pictures. One minute we're on the St Just with Boyd, officially the 'Navigator' but in reality the Captain on the 5,000-odd mile return voyage from West Africa, along with the inept Liverpool gang crew, and the psychotic drunk Ronnie sitting in the wheelhouse with a double-barrelled shotgun waiting to blow off any trespassing head. The next we're in the "Bar L" scrapping with the cons, hearing about the disgusting penal system and the world of the "ungodly", as Boyd puts it.

It's surprising how interesting the prison life chapters are. I thought I would want to skip to the adventures at sea - the great "one ton cannabis run" - but I found the prison world almost more real, and equally fascinating. There is plenty of philosophising about the system and what Keen thinks is wrong. But one would expect no less from a sensitive, caring human being who has been to the bottom of the pit and risen from it. Boyd Keen is now a hero. He made a mistake, he admits it, and he gave a good fight. He won the respect of 'hardmen', 'screws' and Governors of prisons alike. And he's still fighting - now for his life, which is disintegrating from that 20th century disease - the big "C". Ironically, he made the grade to "C" prisoner before his last-minute parole from H M Noranside only 8 months before his sentence was out. Eight years' hard labour, served five, full time.

A brilliant sequence of prison conversational snatches interspersed with the lines of 'Song sung blue' reads like a litany out of the bowels of hell. The lyrical rhythm puts us into a trance where we're inside the prison walls and almost getting used to this horrific yet obsessive way of life. Another striking passage tells of Boyd's feeling for the sea and the boat, how this is what enticed him to take on a dangerous gamble. It wasn't the money, just the chance to go to sea. Boyd writes:

> Ships know not, neither do they care, of the ethics and morals of mankind. Ships do not die of shame, they die of the careless hand of man that puts them in the position that kills them . . . but it is always the hand of man that guides them, feels for them. Understands them. Is at one with them. Ships have a mystic communication with such men... And I knew that I would go with her . . . to what was perhaps my last adventure, my last sea voyage . . .

After 8 months at sea (mostly hanging around sleazy African ports waiting for the Nigerians to get the dope together), it seemed an ironic anticlimax to get done in by the fuzz at an obscure anchorage on the West Coast - Phuilladobhrain - on the island of Seil near Oban. At the same time, perfect. "Easy money? They gotta be joking!"

It's a damn good book, a refreshing break from the neat, tailored poetry that literary connoisseurs are so fond of having for breakfast. In fact, it's better than taking drugs.

Our Lady of the Pickpockets is a deceptive book. It carries a lot of magic, but you have to wait for it, even dig a little. For various reasons I found the first volume of short stories by Dilys Rose hard to get into. But by the time I was half-way through, I began to savour the understated brilliance of the words, the ironies of life she captures so succinctly. Dilys Rose is a young Glasgow writer and a natural crafter of words. Her stories of displacement, of sad and strange people on the edge of the society she encountered on travels in America and Mexico, are told in near 'haiku' fashion, honed down to essential idioms of conversation. Perhaps the title story, 'Our Lady of the Pickpockets', about a 10-year-old Mexican beggar girl who has learned street-wisdom from her mentor named Angel, is the perfect example of the Dilys Rose style in action.

My favourite is 'Self-Portrait, Laughing', the story of an unrecognised painter whose fame is realised only after his death - a heart-rending story which is familiar, as most are in a strange way. Dilys Rose has since won the Macallan/*Scotland on Sunday* short story competition, and is on her way to being one of Scotland's top writers, so it seems. *Our Lady* opened my eyes to a delightful, impish and clever writer whose work is both an inspiration and a revelation to a would-be writer. Distillation is the essence of pure genius. The whisky distilleries have got that one right too.

Gay Hunter is one of the strangest, most beautiful books I've ever read. By contrast, *Blooding Mister Naylor* is one of the worst. I found Boyce's prose and central character offensive, male-ego-obsessive and on a purely materialistic level. This "political thriller cum whodunnit set in and around the "new" Glasgow" is a potboiler all about a yuppie lawyer named Jackie Naylor who defends a peace camp girl wrongly accused of murder and gets into a lot of high-falutin bullshit because of it. It wasn't very well written. Frankly I didn't bother finishing it.

Conversely, *Gay Hunter* is a hidden masterpiece. One of Lewis Grassic Gibbon's science fiction pieces, inspired by H G Wells, according to Edwin Morgan's excellent introduction, the book is a "scientific romance". While romance was the glue which made Gibbon's *A Scots Quair* one of the most memorable trilogies in Scottish literature, romance is only a whiff in the chilling story of post-apocalyptic England 20,000 years ahead in time. Gay Hunter is a young American archaeologist who gets caught up with a Fascist older couple who undertake a psychological experiment and dream themselves into the future. The world has reverted to primitive stone-age society after the holocaust, and the great city of London is now a desolate ruinous dangerous jungle full of giant rats and packs of dogs, but no human life.

As I was reading it, I was travelling to New York, and it was the eeriest experience to be in a place that seemed exactly what was described in Gibbon's 1934 novel, although it was the end of 1990 and the city was intact. His story was so vivid that it was a short imaginative step to see what it could be in 20,000 years. There has been much fiction written about nuclear holocaust, almost to the point of boredom, but *Gay Hunter* is written from a different perspective and time, not laced with the heavily charged atmosphere of fear that pervaded the peace camp protest era in the Cold War '80s. A stunning book, not to be missed.

Marianna Lines

The Chapman New Writing Series...

Singing Seals - Gordon Meade (£5.95+40p p&p)
A genuine poet with a quiet yet insistent voice, he has been blessed with an ability to catch the lyrical moment - *Trevor Royle*

Sting - George Gunn (£5.95+40p p&p)
Here is a man aware, awake, sensible to the hell in which we live, and among all the cross-currents of a crazy world he fights back - *Tom Scott*

The Gangan Fuit - Ellie McDonald (£4.95+40p p&p)
Many of the poems are a development of the Scots lyric tradition, but there is not a hint here of false sentimentality... Joyfully vigorous poems - *Duncan Glen*

Chapman Publications...

Diary of a Dying Man - William Soutar (£4.95+40p p&p)
Not to be confused with Scott's 1954 selection, this is the first time a complete edition of a Soutar diary has been published. With marginalia and illustrations.

Chapman 35-36: The State of Scotland (£4.50+50p p&p)
A predicament for the Scottish writer? A dynamic debate on culture in Scotland.

Chapman Subscriptions...

£9.50 (1 year) £18 (2 years); Institutions £11.50/£22
Overseas: £11/$21 (1 yr) £21/$40 (2 yrs); Institutions £12.50/£24 ($24/$45)

Chapman... 4 Broughton Place, Edinburgh EH1 3RX, Scotland

POETRY WALES

Don't miss our special issue on the
POETRY OF SCOTLAND
featuring poems by Edwin Morgan, Norman MacCaig, Jackie Kay, George Mackay Brown, Alan Bold, William Neill, Robert Crawford, W N Herbert, Tessa Ransford, Iain Crichton Smith, Sheena Blackhall, Davie Purves and many more.

Articles: Ian Gregson on Morgan's Sceptical Nationalism, Christopher Whyte on the Gaelic Renaissance, Tom Hubbard on recent poetry in Scots.

Subscriptions - £8.00 for 4 issues
Individual copies - £1.95 + 50p p&p
Poetry Wales
Andmar House, Tondu Road
Bridgend, Mid-Glamorgan, Wales

SCOTTISH SLAVONIC REVIEW 16

"The Magic Flute"
Bohumil Hrabal
W. D. Dick's
Russian Diary 1828
Bohemian Composers
Refurbishing Europe's
Largest Hotel

Russian poetry in Scots by Edwin Morgan; Polish translations by Donald Pirie; Special feature:- Chekhoviana 1990-1991

Reviews, reports, announcements, illustrations

Subscription £12 (2 issues annually)
Single copies £6; conc £3.95

Dept of Slavonic Languages and Literatures
University of Glasgow, Glasgow G12 8QQ
tel 041 330 5587/5418 fax 041 339 1119

POEMS FROM GARDEN AND CITY

Outside Eden, Margaret Elphinstone, Sundial Press, £4.95; Second Cities, Donny O'Rourke, Vennel Press, £4.95; Tramontana, Hugh McMillan, Dog and Bone £4.50 (041 959 1367) (future D&B titles issued by Canongate); Ophelia and Other Poems, Elizabeth Burns, Polygon, £6.95.

In Outside Eden, Margaret Elphinstone presents us with a poetry which, although always seeking connections is, as in 'Garden in November'

There was the garden on one hand
And you, the man . . .
You seemed small and contained
Under the wind-tossed trees
But necessary for a woman in Eden
Trying to recapture dimension

aware of the risks involved in commitment, and the pain of loss. Here is, indeed, "a vegetable love", extending from the garden, so often the starting point for her poems, to encompass many aspects of the human. For her, both physical and historical/archaeological roots are of great importance; "Go gack, and dig a little/ Among the tattered images and broken dead./ You make those dry bones live" ('Garden in the Ruins').
Her consciousness is "green". but not naive. Eden is a complex of many difficult and sometimes conflicting emotions. "Touch try to touch it is not hard to touch", she tells us in 'Azaleas near Innerleithen', but then warns us in 'Roots', "Touching roots/ is agony / Trees die/ of the commitment/ They cannot break." She is proud of her concern for environment, both physical and psychological, but aware of the dangers of propagating Nature, "I tread carefully/ for fear of crushing anything green/ Which I do not like to do/ Even when it is taking me over" ('September Herb Garden'), and of the dangers gardens may contain, "Things from the dark dragged up by light./ I am the mad gardener./ I love my garden/ Fearfully" ('The Mad Gardener'). Mad gardener or not, hers is a spell of some power. Few who read this, her first collection, are likely to agree when she says. "They will call me mad, and break me/ When I say/ I have more power in these two hands/ Than they ever dreamed of" ('Her Spell').

As Donny O'Rourke's blurb for Second Cities admits, these poems were "meant to be nothing more than one outsider's first impressions. impressionistically set down." However, although some poems betray the fact, again acknowledged by O'Rourke himself, that they "were written quickly" over a period of time in which the poet "slept hardly at all", in the poems that come off, the vitality of the writing is part of their strength. The collection as a whole captures the events and feelings that can occur when one is living at a certain level of awareness, often brought on by a kind of exhaustion when, with one's inhibitions quashed, one finds oneself opened up to different ways of seeing. There are times when all one has to do, as a writer, is to listen, observe and record.
To do this well, one needs a good ear and a keen eye. Much in Second Cities suggests that Donny O'Rourke has both. To quote Margaret Elphinstone's poem 'Potato Cuts', "Impressions should be contained". This is certainly the case in Donny O'Rourke's neat observations of Chicago. Time and again, one remembers odd, striking images: "the shirts blooming in 'Independence Day', and the "asphalt bubbling/ like molasses, manhole covers/ sneezing steam" in 'Daley Bread'. Pervading the collection is his pin-pointing wit, as in 'Frozen Music', "The city burned down and the elevator was invented", and in 'Studs', "at your microphone you keep the 'ago' in Chicago". This is travel writing with a difference. Again, from 'Independence Day': "This room's on the twenty-third floor/ with a full view of the Lake. I absorb that/ and this silver cocktail, thinking of a novice,/ wishing I had a vow." On the strength of this collection, Donny O'Rourke must have put himself in line for a travel bursary, which may lead to more 'Letters from America'.

If Second Cities is an outsider's first impression of a place, Tramontana is an insider's exploration, giving studied observations of a rural locality, the sense of a living place, its bars, people, landscape. Perhaps the less glamorous location - Dumfries is no Chicago - has to do with Hugh McMillan's need for no "special effects" in use of language or metaphor. But the poems' deceptive simplicity is their strength. The first two, 'The Plot Unfolds' and 'A Very Small Miracle', give McMillan at his best. The first, keenly observed, moves smoothly towards the understated crescendo of the dogs' "very small print". Likewise, in the next, simplicity of language allows generosity of spirit to shine through, which shows again in McMillan's observations of people. Even the wit of "life was not a bed of turnips" is gentle, but telling nonetheless. Observations of bar life is another area in which McMillan excels. 'The Station Bar' with its excellent first stanza and crisp ending, and 'Saturday in the Western Bar' with its world "pared down to beer", are two of my favourites.

Two themes interwine in the strong poem 'Willie': McMillan's interest in human strengths and weaknesses, and his concern for geography, or topography - "His face is a map/ and like all landscapes/ is variable./ Willie hasn't always been good./ I think he predates such concepts./ He is both sides of a very old coin./ The man is Galloway." This landscape/mindscape theme is first hinted at in 'The Triumph of the Air', in "the patchwork frazzle of Edinburgh" and his Gran's "carpet like an ocean", and is continued in poems about childhood, his own, his son's and those of schoolchildren, like the tragic 'Tommy'. A more physical feel for landscape is explored in 'Barrhead', 'On the Solway', and 'More Than Geography' which avers: "I'm juddering through arteries of rock./ Going home is more than geography:/ It's tracing the outline of a well loved face/ with the fingers, again, of a child".

In *Ophelia and Other Poems*, Elizabeth Burns' desire for connection is universal, and her universe a feminine one: the first poem is 'Sisters'. The telepathy of sisterhood alluded to dominates it as a whole, from Saint Catherine, through the victims/survivors of South America, to Sylvia Plath, Georgia O'Keefe, and an alcholic's wife. Burns, like Elphinstone, is interested in bones, archaeology. She finds 'Saint Catherine's Monastery' "A place of bones" where "Catherine's herself lie safely fleshless/ shrined in a blue box in her own chapel." However, it is in the excellent 'Gold of the Pharoahs: its discovery' that her interest bears special fruit, where, after being desecrated, the land "lies empty, sterile, her womb/ scraped out as bare as any other in this/ sandblown childless place/ of tombs and bones" Here, indeed, is a sisterhood of the earth.

Again, in 'Colonizers', landscape is feminine, and under threat. The colonisers "will take the hills and glens/ burn the houses/ rape the women/ trample the crofts". 'Autumn in the Graveyard' alludes to more "symbols of women", but it is in the brilliant sequence 'South America: Dreams and Fears' that we first see Burns use women themselves as symbols to great effect. In 'Ophelia', Hamlet's words "clang" in the heroine's head, and in poems about Sylvia Plath and Georgia O'Keefe, Burns allies herself with two artists sympathetic to Shakespeare's character: one whose words come humming "from a churchyard's/ damp chrysanthemums' ('At Plath's Grave'); the other we see making "icons on canvas/ of this bleached landscape/ with infinite wings" ('O'Keefe's Summer'). In the final poem, 'These sands, this shore', Burns finds her landscape of freedom, a place where she can share "things that will ease with the telling/ with the walking on sand/ the soft inrushes of sea". "Here/ where the past is not smothered/ but breathes" we are told that "the heart grows softer being washed like a shell." Yet even in this gentle lyricism, the very landscape of sand and sea will not let us forget the women from 'South America: Dreams and Fears', for whom "a beach is only freedom/ when you have known its opposite/ and have ceased to be afraid". Gordon Meade

NEW FICTION

It Might Have Been Jerusalem, Thomas Healy, £5.95; *Bannock*, Ian McGinness, £7.95; *Leeds to Christmas*, John Cunningham, £7.95, All Polygon; *A Fallen Land*, Janet Broomfield, The Bodley Head, £13.95.

It Might Have Been Jerusalem is a novel of fifties Glasgow about poverty, despair and violence. Bound up in this dismal scenario are the four prominent characters of Anton, Rab, Violet and Rubberneck. Each exists inside their own individual narrative, one story never overlapping with the others; the novel given structural unity by the overwhelming sense of decay, betrayal and uniform grey Glasgow backdrop.

The work functions like an old snapshot album. The action is relayed to us in fragmented pieces. Like instant pictures of a Polaroid camera, we see what has happened to Violet, learn what has been happening to Rab, and so on. This keeps the novel's pace moving but misses out other details and nuances which provide character motivation, insight and create emotional bonds between reader and protagonist. Like an ageing album, the contents become increasingly fetid. Vileness follows Healy's creations around. Rab is plagued in the toilet where "a rat had bit his arse", suffers from other forms of rectal chaos not to mention the attentions of his grotesque wife. Rubberneck is mentally subnormal, Violet unknowingly lends her name to her best friend for use at a VD clinic, the list of atrocities growing longer.

Verging on melodrama, this horrible bombardment has the effect of reducing any feeling for the sorrows of the characters and any interest in the Glasgow of a different era is negated. Healy's work wallows in an excess that ultimately alienates the reader and pales in the shadow of works like *Last Exit to Brooklyn* by Hubert Selby Jr which have trodden similar and more significant paths.

A chirpy, if not wholly cheerful change is offered by Ian McGinness in his second novel, *Bannock*. In perky style McGinness pokes fun at everything he touches. Through the eyes of an adult Adrian Mole figure, George Weems, the town of Bannock - known affectionately as "God's Whelk" by its inhabitants - comes under comic inspection. One of those small historical towns where people constantly hark back to the past to make a living in the present, yet as George finds out, all in Bannock is not as twee and tourist-friendly as an outsider might suppose.

Rivalries and petty jealousies riddle the town and the glorious customs and legendary yores resemble reproduction furniture in not being authentic. As Weems muddles his way through

Bannock's ale houses and tangled histories, he thinks back on his life, a process which creates little hope for his place in the history books. In these tongue-in-cheek flashbacks of Weems' past McGinness's comic vision is at its best. The delusions that Weems has cherished about both his childhood and redundant marriage are both funny and significant. McGinness draws a subtle parallel between the false appraisals of both Weems' and Bannock's past that enables Weems to start afresh. Confident and gently amusing, *Bannock* is an entertaining read but its whimsical nature which means that it is only as funny as the reader's mood allows it to be, lacking that rarer quality of forcing you to laugh despite yourself.

From the land of "big woolly jumpers and stale buns" John Cunningham in *Leeds to Christmas* focusses on the subdued town of Gledhill in South-West Scotland. Here, returning from a lost job in Leeds, 19-year-old Michael starts over again. Michael is lucky and finds lodgings and a new occupation - but with them come various albatrosses. The family he lodges with makes him feel an outsider, despite offering genuine hospitality. His job confines his spirit: All too loudly, the sounds of complacency beckon him.

These pressures are sensitively portrayed by Cunningham in this quiet yet persistent first novel. The pace is slow and some of Michael's thoughts, especially regarding his furtive encounters with his landlady, seem too careful for a young man who in other ways lacks maturity. Such cracks make *Leeds to Christmas* slightly stilted and cloyed, flawing an otherwise promising work.

Another first novel is *Fallen Land* by Janet Broomfield, set in Victorian Edinburgh - a city divided by the New Town's dazzling wealth and the crippling poverty of the Old Town. Helen Lambert is lives in the New Town and Lizzie Crearie sadly in the latter. The disparities between the lives of these characters is admirably managed and makes a memorable account of life in old Edinburgh. Eventually the pair find that their paths cross and intermingled with all the trappings of thwarted love and social misunderstandings the book reaches a happy ending.

This work is more than a standard historical romance, despite the prerequisite fumbles between the sexes: "her clothes seemed . . . an unnatural barrier . . . he pressed urgently against her" The book is a tribute to historical research, wedged full of suspense, social conscience and containing even a latent feminism. Broomfield's work is principled, evocative, tender and convincing: a worthy recipient of the Historical Novel Prize in Memory of Georgette Heyer. Walking down The Royal Mile will never be the same again.

Sara Evans

Kisties

Aa breenge in! Rebel Scottish Songs and Poems - a tribute to Morris Blythman, £6.00, Gallus/- SFUTB, GAL109; *Songs from Under the Bed No 3*; £4.00; *Songs from Under the Poll Tax*, £1.50 both SFTUB; all from John Greig, 37 Claremont Bank, Edinburgh 7; *William Neill: Poems in the Thrie Leids o Alba*, SSC 089, £5.25 inc p&p, Scotsoun, 13 Ashton Rd, Glasgow 12.

These cassettes are linked by their non-commercial origins. Their producers are motivated not by desire to make fortunes, but admiration for the writers or belief in a political cause. Costs have been kept down by cutting recording time or using volunteer performers rather than highly-paid recording stars. It may be argued that although a singer fluffs a word or a reader a line of poetry, the work survives unimpaired. So it does, for those who know and love the material, but may not win over new listeners accustomed to the polished results of professional production.

I cannot excise nostalgia from my appreciation of *Aa Breenge In*, though what do 25-year-old listeners make of songs full of references from before their birth - the Gaitskell "Peanuts" speech, the reiving o the Stane, the CND campaign against Polaris? I remember when everybody was singing these songs in folk clubs. Among listeners then were those assembled for this recording: the traditional style of Andy Hunter in his understated but intense "Twa Corbies"; the entertaining impudence of Alastair MacDonald: the clear singing of Susan Ross, the Glasgow growl of Jimmy Ross and the idiosyncratic delivery of Ewan MacVicar, who makes the 'Ballad of John McCorbie' sound like early Peter Nardini.

The inclusion of the poems in non-Glaswegian Scots, read by Joy Hendry and Raymond Ross. shows how favourite images such as the roulette wheel occur whatever mode Morris wrote in. It also leads to speculation: what if he had developed the poetry instead of protest song? The range of Morris's musical models and the campaigns he wrote for is clear. Surprisingly, the important Swing to the SNP campaign in Pollok is omitted. *Swing* is also missing from some of the renditions. The performers seem nervous of the Orange tunes, and *breenge* through them instead of giving them the swagger Morris admired. So Ian Davison sings 'The Scottish Breakaway' with fast American guitar accompaniment and nobody joining the chorus, and when the 'Eskimo Republic' cries out for a jaunty flute or whistle, there wanders in a forlorn fiddle, like an improvised studio addition. In contrast, Alastair MacDonald's arrangements are carefully-thought-out:

perky multi-tracked banjo on 'Perfervidum Ingenium', and a soulful guitar on 'Superintendent Barratt' - as cheeky as Morris could have asked for. The interplay between different moods of tune and text was a frequent source of humour for Morris Blythman. He loved the irony of using well-known American tunes for songs against American occupation of the Holy Loch.

The singer/song-writers of *Songs from Under the Poll Tax* could learn from that. Their renditions match their models too closely. Their nice blues and calypso remain nice blues and calypso; they do not become ironic Scottish protest songs. More successful was the 'Poll Tax Rap', but rap has been over-used recently. *Songs from Under the Bed No 3* again has the advantage of variety, featuring five writers.

Freddy Anderson knows what is wrong in the world and has fought against it in verse and prose all his life. The selection of poems here, however, makes me ask why his prose is more precise and incisive than his poetry. When he chooses a come-all-ye framework it works well enough, but when he selects a tighter form, too often rhyme and rhythm are allowed to slip. Though Freddie isn't the greatest elocutionist, it is good to hear the poems spoken naturally in the accent for which they were created. I might have said the same about Stephen Shellward's songs had he not overlaid his Ulster accent with a Dylan-style drawl though his narratives, particularly the experienced detail of 'Dog Man', have the power to hold the listener. Dylan has also left his mark on Ewan MacVicar. "The Highlands are weeping, the Lowlands will drown" is typical post-Dylan catch-all symbolism. However, Ewan's very personal 'Ga's Song' is the best on the tape and the one most likely to be sung by others. Jim Ferguson also was better with a personal song about his father than in an American-influenced international protest song.

Jim Milligan could learn both from Morris Blythman and Ewan MacVicar. His live set made his audience nervous about whether his bad rhymes were intentional or not. He should either, like Morris, point up his worst excesses with pauses for the audience to think "surely he's not going to rhyme CIRCUS with CHRISTMAS!" or, like Ewan, sing confidently as if he believed that FRONT and UP rhymed perfectly. Alternatively, he could work harder and improve his rhymes.

Lack of discipline cannot be charged against William Neill. He is a proud poetic craftsman whether working in Gaelic, Scots or English. As the title suggests all three languages are featured on the tape, Gaelic taking up most of side two. Though he has many poetic voices - comic, lyrical, philosophical - Neill speaks naturally in all three tongues in the same voice, in a tone suggesting resigned melancholy. In comparison, some of the other readers sound as if they are putting on a reading voice. Their contributions, however, are valuable. the measured pace of Josephine Neill, George Philp or Kenneth Mac-Donald has advantages for the first-time listener unfamiliar with some of the words. Melancholy Neill may be about the state of the nation and its languages; resigned he is not. He continues to speak out for the culture he sees threatened in poems of pith, wisdom and beauty. This tape gives such a fine selection that it is good value even for those with only one of the languages.

Adam McNaughtan

Theatre Roundup

Possibly the last-minute dropping-out of Nigel Kennedy lifted the music side of things; but as regards drama, this year's Festival was one of the most disappointing in memory. This was firstly on account of various dashed expectations, such as the cancellation of *Peter Pan*, and a Ninegawa production which fell far below the tremendous standards of previous offerings. This would have mattered less had there been anything outstanding amongst the rest of the drama, but there simply wasn't. And since this was Frank Dunlop's last Festival, one was hoping he might exit on a crescendo of triumph, cocking genial farewell snoots at critics and councillors alike. That the reverse happened was possibly the most doleful and disappointing of all.

Tango at the End of Winter, which is by a contemporary Japanese writer, is the first work Ninegawa has directed in English. Perhaps he should have kept it in the original, or perhaps it's just a bad play; set in an old cinema destined to make way for a supermarket, it features a morose middle-aged actor beset by a number of mid-life crises, and tiers upon tiers of symbolism. The symbolism, in fact, is so dense and high-piled that much of it appears to refer merely to other, equally impenetrable symbols. Are the cardboard silhouettes there to keep Sei from feeling lonely, or are they to drop some grander hint about the emptiness of interpersonal relationships? And if anyone knows, does it matter anyway? Ninegawa's *Macbeth* (1985) and *Medea* (1986) will be remembered for decades by all who saw them; but on this occasion, sadly, the magic failed.

The most interesting of the rest of a decidedly mixed bunch was provided by the Moscow Lenkom company with *Too Clever By Half*. The prolific 19th-century dramatist Alexander Ostrovsky is given the occasional tentative airing in this country, but not usually a production as alarmingly and violently creative as this one which, if nothing else, achieved a degree of minor fame for the array of chandeliers so large that you could act in them. The play itself is a kind of onion-skin parable, in which an ambitious schemer simultaneously sucks up to and exposes the mores and prejudices of genteel society. There was certainly plenty of energy, but I felt that too often the message was being presented in large bold capitals, heavily underlined and then highlighted with a fluorescent marker to boot; some measure of restraint would have been welcome. Nevertheless it should be added that there were many who enjoyed it unreservedly.

And now to the Scottish plays. For many years, there have been scattered but strident voices calling for R S Silver's play *The Bruce* to be given a full-scale professional production. Well, now they've had their Bannockburn, so to speak; and I hope they all took advantage of the opportunity to see this deeply-pondered, impeccably tasteful and thoroughly moral work at least half-a-dozen times, for some of us wouldn't mind at all not being reminded of it for a good while to come.

Yet at least some merit of comparative novelty attached to *The Bruce*; more than can be said for *The Thrie Estates* which was dragged creaking and unkempt out of decent oblivion to do service as a stop-gap replacement for Bill Bryden's cancelled *Peter Pan*. The funny Scots accents were dusted off: so were numbers of funny hats in the wardrobes of the matrons of Marchmont and Morningside; and a genteel time was had by all.

I know that *Thrie Estates* is a powerful and original work of high literary talent, and that properly done (which would almost certainly require a new text and generous quantities of money and inspiration, neither of them commodities in easy supply at the moment) it could make marvellous theatre; and again, I understand exactly why Dunlop felt he had to do a Burke-and-Hare on it.

We come here to what I feel has been quite a bugbear for non-Scottish Festival directors; coming from outside, they invariably encounter carping about locals not being chosen, and naturally try to prove their commitment by putting on things with a Scottish angle.

In the case of Frank Dunlop, this has been very marked; but the man who in the last eight years has brought some amazing World Theatre seasons to Edinburgh has had more than a little difficulty finding good Scottish work suitable for an international audience. True, there have been at least a couple of successes over the years - I, at any rate would unequivocally consider the Brunton's *Holy Isle* and Communicado's *Danton* as such - but there has also been much that has been unashamedly dire. One thinks of Hywel Bennett as Long John Silver, looking rather sicker than his parrot; of a drear and draughty version of Schiller's *Mary Queen of Scots* at the Assembly Hall; of Iain Heggie's dismal and dated *Clyde Nouveau* at the Churchill.

But it is not on such a note that a valediction to Frank Dunlop should end. He has done magnificent things for the Festival, and given abundant pleasure; and for my part, I shall remember his reign not only for the block-busters (of which there were more than a few), but even more for the many smaller shows that gave exquisite and often unlooked-for delight. Picking at random, these would include such gems as Deschamps' spell-binding paean to love and eld, *C'est Dimanche*; Miriam Margolyes' *The Women in Dickens*, with its vivid assortment of character-sketches: a thrillingly fresh *Hedda Gabler* from New Zealand: or Gunter Grass's *The Double Bass*, a wonderful duologue between an unregarded musician and his unregarded instrument, brilliantly performed by an actor of whom I had never previously heard.

Remembering shows like these, I find it impossible to share in the silly row that blew up when Dunlop made - albeit perhaps not very well - a serious point about the Fringe becoming more difficult for good new drama, which was subsequently misunderstood by the Provost and then needlessly blown up by the media. It was a sad and souring affair, but not one that detracts from the fine record of his eight years as director.

So, emphatically well done Frank; and the more so. since all was accomplished under conditions of grisly adversity. This year these included having to do without a major theatre, because of some bijou problemettes in the refurbishment of the Lyceum. (And having seen the distressingly tacky new Lyceum since, I wish they had left the front just as it was. However, since on the evidence of the numbing inaugural production of *An Ideal Husband* the Lyceum company has returned from its near-hibernation not with recharged batteries but merely to enter on a new lease of lifelessness. perhaps I shan't be seeing too much of the Dodge City decor.)

Returning to the theme. however. after that intemperate digression: the upshot of the delays with the Lyceum was that hasty arrangements were made to open the Empire Theatre. It was wonderful to see this splendid venue in use as a theatre: and if it was still rank with the aura of bingo, if tatty stacked chairing was in requisition and grimy plastic sheeting was swathed around - well it's what visitors to the International Festival have come to expect, isn't it?

The question of venues has long been pressing; the Playhouse is frankly not suitable for anything more serious than Kylie Minogue, and regarding St Bride's one can only say that whilst working on a shoestring is one thing, performing in a shoebox is quite another. However, at the time of writing, the People's Republic of Edinburgh, stupendously, has declared its commitment to a budget of £15 million to transform the Empire and make it the best opera house in Britain. We shall see.

The new director of the Festival is Brian McMaster; I'm sure we all wish him luck, for he will certainly need it. He will also need a stout plated corselet, for Festival directors tend to get stabbed in the front as well as the back.

Alasdair Simpson

Pamphleteer

I fancy a trip to the astral plane some time, but the travel agents are unreliable. Meantime, there are holiday snaps in the form of *Scientary*, part of Eric Ratcliffe's project, *The Experiment* (Astrapost, 92b High Street, Old Town, Stevenage, Herts SG1 3DW; £1): Theosophical poetry which takes in ghosts, *zeitgeists*, good sense and "somewhere perhaps is Einstein in his grace,/ ensouled and guiding new Aquarian schemes,/ vibrating rubrics into curving space,/ who thought the Lord was subtle, not malicious." *Hill 60* (also from *The Experiment*, £1.50 from the same address) ranges similarly with its warlike theme, while back on earth, Ratcliffe's engaging, though hideously-produced, *Ballad of Polly McPoo* (£2.00) is a gentle lampoon of the literary world.

Still on the astral plane, it's disappointing that David Gray's *In the Shadows* (Hearing Eye, Box 1, 99 Torriano Ave, London NW5 2RX, £3.50) is printed and published in London since it's SAC funded and Gray himself was born near Kirkintilloch. John Heath-Stubbs has rescued this collection of sonnets by a young man coming to terms with TB at the age of 23, which appeared shortly after Gray's death in 1862. The influence of Keats is prominent, and the young man's conceit that he might one day be buried in Westminster Abbey is not without foundation.

Closer to home, *Two Streets and a Castle* is a collection of short stories from the Perseverance Writers' Club (14 Drumbrae Ave, Edinburgh EH12 8TE, £2.95). There's some strong material here, including 'Three Weeks in August', Ann Hay's convincing account - if that's not too pointy-fingered a word - of a brief fling, and Bill Lennox's riotous 'Craighorn and the Belfast Poker' in which the women in the village of Craighorn - to a person, it seems - are charmed out of their cash and kecks by an Irishman posing as a fortune-teller. "Every child born for the next six months would be treated with suspicion..." and the local JP, before whose court the Irishman's case is heard, subsequently takes on the guise of a gypsy before being run out of town.

Duncan McLean is producing likeable stuff from the Clocktower Press, 17 West Terrace, South Queensferry EH30 9LL. For a quid apiece there's his own *The Druids Shite It, Fail To Show*, where a group of Casuals gather at a neolithic site to ponder life and build cairns of lager-cans. With James Meek he's written *Safe/Lurch*. Fergus is a worried man and wants to go on holiday: "'To be totally honest with you,' said Fergus, 'I'm a bit disappointed with the choice of countries.' 'That's a map of the world. That's all the countries there are.'"; Lurch can't walk straight. Then there's *Zoomers*, very short stories (21 in 20 pages) by McLean, Meek, Legge and others.

Much of the material in *Setting Forth* (Rivet Publishing, 12 East Terrace. South Queensferry, West Lothian EH30 9HS) has appeared elsewhere, but has been collected together by Mark Meredith as part of the celebrations for the Forth Rail Bridge Centennial. It's an appropriate idea, since healthy numbers of distinguished writers live or have lived in South Queensferry. Among those represented in the book are Sydney Goodir Smith, Andrew Greig, Kathleen Jamie and Hector Macmillan. I particularly liked Ron Butlin's 'Preparations for a Sea Voyage': "It was like this: we made the spare oars/ from wax; the ropes from weed;/ smoke we gathered into sails, and the prow/ was once the concentration of a cat..."

Among the stories of sheepdogs and other aspects of everyday life gathered in *Jaunts and Jottings* (Gorebridge Women's Writing Group) there's one couplet in tutor Howard Purdie's 'Friendly Bombs' which captures the deadly absurdity of the so-called 'smart warfare' waged in the Gulf earlier in the year: "... At our door politely knocks./ And asks if we are Number Nine?/ And if we are - explodes on time." *Anthem* no 7 (The Rand Society of Poets, c/o 36 Cyril Ave, Bobber's Mill, Nottingham NG8 5BN,) asks questions (but not, it has to be said, too well) about personal responsibility vis à vis the state, among other things with reference to AIDS: "In this wasted town/ I've seen a million things/ come and go/ And those that stay/ Just wither and die/ Like flowers from the den of iniquity." ('Holes in the Wall'). The issue's dedication to Kate Bush "(and yes, Kate, we are all completely mad!!!!)" is neither funny or helpful.

Painful questions are more convincingly addressed in Patricia Pogson's *Rattling the Handle* (Littlewood Arc. Nanholm Centre. Shaw Wood

Road, Tormorden, Lancs OL14 6DA, £5): "One day she came back/ from whatever it was/ to find me bleeding./ He told me I'd sat/ on a piece of wood/ with a nail sticking out. . . Every time he touched me/ I disappeared a little more" ('Walls'). There are happier sides to Pogson and a dignity about the collection as a whole, as with Littlewood Arc's other new book, *Grandfather Best and the Protestant Work Ethic* by John Ward. A mixture of biography and observation, these poems show a vigour which belies the author's 70 years (I assume the poet is talking about himself in 'Great-Uncle John, 1858-1911'). For example, 'The Hallelujah Tariff', lampooning American mass-media religion: "Fifty dollars, and the Reverend Joe/ will pray for you on his radio show./ Five hundred, and the Reverend Max/ will explain to God about your income tax . . ."

It is unfortunate that the rhymes in Charles Edward Stuart's *Selected Poems* (Golden Fleece Press, 63 Barshaw Rd, Penilee, Glasgow G52 4EE, £3.50) are so indigestible e.g. "Once I had a dream of my lady love fair,/ I dreamt I appeared to her debonair", ('To Reality') because the sentiments contained in the poetry are far from worthless. Without wishing to seem patronising, Stuart could learn a lot from the craftsmanship in Gordon Meade's *Walking Towards the Sea* (Villa Vic Press, 11 Newminster Rd, Newcastle NE4 9LL). This contains more recent material than his *Chapman* collection *Singing Seals*, more of his concentrated passion: "Imagine a bird,/ Once a pirate in blacks,/ Now a beggar in a clotted sack./ And don't imagine it, see it,/ Approach it,/ Get within six feet of it./ Then, see it try to open plastered/ wings and fly. See it fail," ('A Cormorant in Oils').

Like the Desmond Graham collections. *Walking Towards the Sea* is a signed, limited edition with illustrations by Chris Daunt. Desmond Graham's *A Rumtopf for Summer* is a bit rich for my taste, but there's some nice fruit in it. Poor Desmond's out of luck: I don't much care for Chopin's preludes either - 19th century composers' fondness for the title 'Prelude' has always struck me as oxymoronic since nothing ever comes *after* them except more preludes. Of course I'm being grossly unfair to *A Set of Signs for Chopin's Twenty Four Preludes* because things like No 23:

Riverboats, people,
riverboats, moonlight,
when the wind blows
each ripple is starlight.

Riverboats, people,
riverboats, moonlight,
when the wind is still
you could walk from bank
to bank on a path of moonlight.

are lovely.

I'm content to wind up on the West Coast with Peter McCarey's *Town Shanties* (Broch Books, 31 Willowbank Crescent, Glasgow G3 6NA, £4.95). If McCarey's flip side doesn't always come off - he makes a crack about breathing life into the OED, for example, when the words he uses I would find in any dictionary worth its salt - he has a flair for vivid imagery: ". . . and the cold of its indifference to you/ lodges like a virus in the ghettoes of your blood." ('Gastarbeit') "Ice makes dice from dalebones . . ." ('Shipley') and there are better jokes. 'Our Leader has a Vision of Judgment before Calling in the Tanks' deals with the Loopy Old Bat's demise last year; 'Year Zero' takes as its text a remark of Richard Dawkins from *The Selfish Gene* about words and definitions, and arrives at "Define means execute/ a means any/ word means terrorist". Containing substantial intellectual breadth and, as Edwin Morgan puts it, "a very Scottish intoxicant of flyting", *Town Shanties* is an impressive debut collection.

Peter Cudmore

Catalogue

The Dipper an the Three Wee Deils by J.A. Begg & J. Reid (Luath Press, £5) presents tales and verse in interesting Ayrshire Scots, at times excellent: 'Craws' has lines its author can be proud of:

Nae mair we pyke oot sodgers' een
Whaur the deid lie gash and pale.
The battlefield was aye oor frien
Whaur craws could pick an wale . . .

. . . man's aye been a wastrife race
An his coups can fill oor wame.

Forbye, we hae his gran new roads
Whaur the speldered deid lie blae:
Hurcheons, mawkins, brocks and tods
Keep us weel fed ilk day.

Sae we can brawly bide oor time
While man gangs on ram-stam . . .

Luath Press also publish *Seven Steps in the Dark*, by Bob Smith (£8.95). Considerable in spirit and to-the-pointness, there is something properly epic about this autobiography of a Scots miner, with striking scenes like a cascade of rats stampeding out a day before comprehensive cave-in, and numerous heroic tales of generations who at fourteen walked by the school gate and if they were lucky 'doun the pit', a curious phrase without Poe-ish resonance as spoken. Like many gifted miners, Bob Smith got involved in union work and safety campaigns, and in the latterday Lanarkshire miner's trawl from one pit to another as they shut. In real respects a tremendous book.

R D S Jack's prodigious reassessment of J M

Barrie's dramatic art, *The Road to the Never Land* (AUP £25) uses a section of Chapter 5 entitled 'A Critical Never Land' to give wise warning of the Modern Scot Lit tendency toward "communication within an inner group about topics of interest to that group alone". He insists rightly on the need for a wider literary base, and throughout this study has clearly in mind various false anticipations, not to say caricatures, which get in the way not only in his paradigm case of Barrie. One need not esteem Barrie greatly (different estimations are strongly challenged) to find acute insight into *Weltanschaüung*, historical-cultural reference, and the real danger of reparochialisation of Scot Lit and Crit.

Tom Crawford's *Boswell, Burns and the French Revolution* (Saltire Society, £3.95) is a vivid account of a happily contrived theme, written with great literary and psychological penetration. Gregory Claeys has produced a useful selection, *A New View of Society & Other Writings* by Robert Owen (Penguin, £6.99), of New Lanark fame. *Man of Letters* ed. C.H. Layman is a reconstruction, from various writings and correspondence of the subsequent publisher Robert Chambers, of a life and times, surviving poverty in Peebles and becoming a literary coach-and-four author and publisher in Edinburgh (EUP £8.95). Latter days are marked by Beat Witschi's comprehensive study of Alasdair Gray's writings *Glasgow Urban Writing and Post-Modernism*, which is well done and not over-constricted by the method its title implies (Peter Lang, DM-70, c.£26)

From Polygon: *Cosmos*, the yearbook of the Traditional Cosmology Society, Vol.6 1990, and the Cosmos series of astonishingly assorted books, including Emily Lyle's most impressive collection of papers *Archaic Cosmos*, Polarity, Space and Time (£7.95), ranging over Roman, Celtic and Chinese among cosmologies, like *Cosmos* itself; *The Euphrates at Babylon* (tr. Richard Aczel, £7.95) by the Hungarian-from-Romania Adam Bodor is a series of stories or sketches quite startlingly visual, and evocative of the by no means archaic land of Ceausescu. *Jan Lobel from Warsaw*, by Luise Rinser, tr. Michael Hulse (£4.99) prints a short novella and a long, interesting interview noting this German writer's devotion to Joseph Conrad.

Walter Perrie's *Roads that Move*, a journey through eastern Europe (Mainstream, £12.99) manages to mention a "mean-spirited Church of Scotland minister" who sponsored a reading by Iosif Brodsky arranged by the author in Edinburgh, but did not satisfy on expenses. Doubtless the sponsors of this book stumped up, though some of many meals reported (a major feature of the book) were donated. Apart from the culinary critique, ornithology, reference book notes on E. European history, Wittgenstein, the Scoto-Irish knittings from which the author emerged. Even for a travel book this does move about a lot. It also affords fascinating and perfectly timed if eccentric insight into the different East and Central European revolutions as, one by one, their communist regimes tumbled.

Symbol and Archetype, by Martin Lings (£17.50/£7.95) defines symbolism as the most important thing in, also the sole explanation of, existence. The publisher Quinta Essentia, at 5 Green Street, Cambridge, shares an address with the Islamic Text Society. Other books received include *The Bloody Brother*, A Tragedy by John Fletcher and Nathan Field and Refurbished by Phillip Massinger as 'Rollo, Duke of Normandy' ed. Bertha Hensman (Vantage, $16.95); *Verne's Journey to the Centre of the Self*, Space and Time in the *Voyages Extraordinaires* by William Butcher (Macmillan, £35); *Because it is my Name*, Problems of identity experienced by women, artists and breadwinners in the plays of Henrik Ibsen, Tennessee Williams and Arthur Miller by Nada Zeineddine (£11.95, Merlin); the mercifully titled *The Poetry of Edward Thomas*, by Andrew Motion (Hogarth, £7.99); Ronald Gaskell's *Wordsworth's Poem of the Mind* on *The Prelude* (EUP £16.95). One book much waited for is *Golgonooza, City of Imagination* (Golgonooza Press, £19.50/£7.95), final book of several devoted (right word) by Kathleen Raine to William Blake. Albion indeed sleepeth, yet some have visions.

Issues of Self-Determination ed. William Twining (AUP £18.95), a series of papers on that theme from the 14th World Congress in Philosophy of Law and Social Philosophy, 1989, justifies further a venture producing 9 volumes of proceedings. J.K. Gillon's richly illustrated *Eccentric Edinburgh* (Moubray House, £6.95) does a great deal to rescue Edinburgh from the 18th century, and reveal the unselfconscious, colourful and happily by no means sane business which is nearer the beating heart of a city of much more than just reason. Rupert Besley's *Scotland for Beginners* (Lochar, £4.95) is Bill MacTidy cartoons. Alas, some illustrations in Hugh Cheape's *Tartan - The Highland Habit* unwittingly cause like mirth (National Museums of Scotland, £5.95). The text slaloms annoyingly between visuals. Handsome of course is George Mackie's *Books & Other Ephemera* (National Library of Scotland £3.50) - the designer of past EUP books tells all and does himself justice with outstanding graphics. *Illustrators in Scotland* is an incredibly various catalogue of work by young active Scots (Graphic Partners, Gladstone Court, 179 Canongate, Edinburgh EH8 8BN).

Notes on Contributors

Tom Bryan, Canadian by birth but of Scottish descent, works on a north-west fish farm having married a Scottish music teacher. Articles, stories, poetry published in *Lines Review, Cencrastus* &c.

Ian Crockatt is a social worker living in Fort William; published in magazines and anthologies once a year for the last 20 years.

Mary Edward lives and teaches in Glasgow. *Who Belongs to Glasgow?* to be published by Glasgow District Libraries shortly.

Nissim Ezekiel: b. 1924 to a Jewish family in Bombay. Former professor of English at Bombay University and India's leading English language poet.

Donald C Farquhar lives in Dunblane and works for the Hydro Electric Board.

Pete Fortune lives & works in Dumfries. Writer of stories & occasional journalism. Denies everything.

Duncan Glen taught Graphic Design &c for many years; distinguished editor of *Akros*. Now resident in Edinburgh, editing his new magazine *Z20*

Joy Hendry, radio critic of *The Scotsman* and writer in residence for Stirling District Council.

Koert Linde is a visual artist and poet, born in the Netherlands, recently returned to Scotland.

Norman MacCaig, poet and philanthrope, making welcome re-acquaintance with his fountain pen after a long silence.

Sorley MacLean, distinguished Gaelic poet, celebrating his 80th birthday at a reading organised by *Chapman* (30th Oct 1991).

Maureen Macnaughtan is a Glaswegian now living in Glenrothes. Poetry in a number of anthologies and such magazines as *Poetry Review* and *Iron*.

Gerry Mangan, (Norman MacCaig cartoons) Scottish poet, artist and journalist, currently living in Paris.

Gordon Meade lives in the East Neuk of Fife. His first full-length collection of poetry, *Singing Seals*, is available now in the *Chapman* New Writers' series.

Mary Montgomery is a radio producer, participant in the annual Irish/Scottish exchange. Publications include *Eadar mi 's a' Bhreug* (Coisceim, Dublin).

Peter Mowat: "I write under a full moon/ in the open air/ as far from civilisation/ as the extension cable/ from my flickering word screen will allow/ until the shilling runs out."

Donald S Murray lives in Stornoway, teaches English. Some day he hopes to write a book.

Sandy Neilson actor/director of long standing in the Scottish theatrical community; founder member, Fifth Estate.

Colin Nicholson lectures in the English Literature dept, Edinburgh University. Editor of a forthcoming book of critical essays on Iain Crichton Smith.

Jack Rillie taught in the English Dept, Glasgow University for many years. Decent, though not diluvial, output of essays, reviews, broadcasts; no space to mention hunting crocodile in Zuarungu.

Gael Turnbull's most recent publication is the lavishly decorated and dreadfully expensive *As from a Fleece*, Circle Press (London).

John Welch, teacher of philosophy at St Louis University Madrid campus; has been published in *Nantucket Review, The Iceman, Visions* and others.